Solitude

Cowley Publications is a ministry of the Society of St. John the Evangelist, a religious community for men in the Episcopal Church. Emerging from the Society's tradition of prayer, theological reflection, and diversity of mission, the press is centered in the rich heritage of the Anglican Communion.

Cowley Publications seeks to provide books, audio cassettes, CDs, and other resources for the ongoing theological exploration and spiritual development of the Episcopal Church and others in the body of Christ. To this end, it is dedicated to developing a new generation of theological writers, encouraging them to produce timely, creative, and stimulating publications of excellence, and making these publications available widely, reaching both clergy and lay persons.

SOLITUDE

A Neglected Path to God

Christopher Chamberlin Moore

COWLEY PUBLICATIONS
Cambridge · Boston
Massachusetts

Published in the United States of America by Cowley
Publications, a division of the Society of St. John the Evangelist.
No portion of this book may be reproduced, stored in or introduced into a retrieval system, or transmitted, in any form or by
any means—including photocopying—without the prior written
permission of Cowley Publications, except in the case of brief
quotations embedded in critical articles and reviews.

Library of Congress Cataloging-in-Publication Data:
Moore, Christopher Chamberlin.
    Solitude : a neglected path to God / Christopher Chamberlin
    Moore.
    p. cm.
    Includes bibliographical references.
    ISBN 1-56101-198-3 (alk. paper)
    1. Solitude—Religious Aspects—Christianity. 2. Spiritual
    Life—Christianity. I. Title.
BV4509.5 .M63 2001
248.4'7—dc21   2001042258

Scripture quotations are taken from *The New Revised Standard
Version* of the Bible, © 1989, by the Division of Christian
Education of the National Council of the Churches of Christ in
the United States of America. Used by permission.

Cynthia Shattuck, editor; Vicki Black, copyeditor and designer
Cover art: John La Farge, *Nelson's Pond from the Puddingstone
Ledge, at Paradise*, c. 1865

This book was printed in Canada on recycled, acid-free paper.

Cowley Publications
28 Temple Place • *Boston, Massachusetts 02111*
800-225-1534 • *www.cowley.org*

TO JANICE,
ALICE, DOUGLAS, AND MOLLY

anchors in my solitude

Contents

Acknowledgments

I wish to thank the members of my congregation, the Church of the Holy Comforter in Drexel Hill, Pennsylvania, who provided fertile ground to develop the ideas in this book, and of my summer congregations, St. Philip's by the Sea, Fortunes Rocks, and St. Martin's in the Field, Biddeford Pool, both in Maine. It was in St. Martin's quiet and sun-filled rectory that this book was born.

I am indebted also to Rob and Karen Kittredge, who generously lent me their home on two occasions for reading, writing, and solitude; to Cynthia Shattuck, director of Cowley Publications, a "hands on" editor whose suggestions, corrections, and gentle proddings have guided this project since its inception; and to my secretary, Rosemarie Williams, who performed the miracle of transforming my illegible scrawls into a completed and legible manuscript.

CHRISTOPHER CHAMBERLIN MOORE

DREXEL HILL, PENNSYLVANIA

CHAPTER ONE

The Loss
of Solitude

This book was born in solitude on a quiet summer morning on the coast of Maine. I had driv-
en up the night before with my twelve-year-old son.
A grueling ten-hour drive skirting the rush hour traffic of Philadelphia, New York, and Boston culminat-
ed in a traffic jam on the Maine Turnpike. By the
time we arrived there, we were exhausted. We
unloaded the van, tumbled into the house, and fell
into bed.

The next morning I awoke to one of those glori-
ous summer days for which Maine is justly famous.
I lay in bed, savoring the silence. After a few moments
I got up and went downstairs. The sun was stream-
ing in through the windows in the direction of the

bay. The silence in the house was palpable. No phone. No doorbell. No traffic sounds. Only the ticking of the clock. I thought of that phrase, the "sounds of silence," from one of my favorite sixties songs.

At that moment I found myself experiencing something that I had not known for some time. It was solitude. My son still asleep upstairs, my wife and daughter not yet due to arrive, I was for the moment alone. And liking it.

The fact is, solitude had played little part in my life during the past year—and more. I was the rector of a large Episcopal church in the suburbs of Philadelphia and a parent of two young people now entering their busy teen years. I was also responsible for members of the older generation of my family. The busy and overloaded nature of my life was not only the result of outer circumstances, however. It was also the result of lifestyle choices I had freely made. Like many people, I had a tendency to take on too much, to never say "no." Shortly before I left for Maine, I had read a passage in a recently published book that cut uncomfortably close to the circumstances of my own life as a priest. It was an account of a conversation over dinner between two busy professional friends, one a well-known doctor who had introduced revolutionary patient-care procedures at his prestigious medical center.

When I remark about the success of his work and ask about its future, his dark eyes suddenly well up with tears! Is he becoming emotional because of the deep feeling he has for his work or his patients? Not exactly. He puts down his cup and in an unsteady voice that is part desperation and part anger he says "I have no time." I nod sympathetically. But he goes on: "You don't understand. I have no time! I am pathologically busy. It's beyond anything I have ever imagined. I can't give anything the attention it needs. I can't do anything well. I wake up in the middle of the night on the verge of a breakdown. And more and more people depend on me. More and more things, good things, important things, keep coming to me. Any one of them is worth the whole of my attention and needs my time. But ten, twenty of them? A hundred of them? And it is the same with my staff. They are all being driven past their limits. . . . " My friend keeps talking, talking. I cannot find a moment to break in to say, "Yes, I understand. It's the same with me."[1]

In this conversation I recognized not only my life, but also the lives of many of my friends and parishioners. I realized that *time* was an element that had been missing from my life. But it was not only time. It was time *alone*. It was *solitude*. And in the same moment I realized that times I had spent alone over the years had been some of the best of my life.

I remembered an evening in the spring of my last year of seminary. For months I had been wrestling with whether or not I should enter the ordained ministry and, if so, what shape that ministry would take. Finally, one evening, it all became clear, and I remember walking for hours in solitude as the shape of my ministry suddenly was revealed to me.

I remembered also a very different evening several years before—one in which I was traveling across the country, alone. I had dinner at a roadside diner in a tiny desert community and crossed the road to return to my motel. The desert sunset was lighting the sky. Drawn by impulse, I walked into the desert. The silence was intense. I found myself slowing down and listening, *really* listening. At one point, I became aware of a tiny rustling sound. Drawn by curiosity, I followed the sound to its source, and discovered two leaves of a dry desert plant rubbing together. What incredible silence, I thought to myself, that I can hear two leaves rubbing together.

As I reflected on these and other experiences over the years, they seemed to have two things in common. One, they had been self-defining experiences. They had brought me back in touch with a sense of who I was—my bedrock values, interests, goals, and sense of calling. As a priest they had revealed to me the shape of my ministry, the particular path of service to which God was calling me. Solitude had allowed me to see through the clutter of my life and regain a sense of clarity. The second characteristic of these experiences was that they were by nature solitary. It was not "too bad" that I had had no one to share them with at the moment. The fact was, I had deliberately sought out these experiences in solitude. They were what they were precisely because they were experienced alone.

As I reflected on these and other experiences over the years, I was aware of two ironies. While some of the best moments of my life had been experienced in solitude, I live in a society that tends to disparage time alone and instead holds up successful relationships as the key to a happy and fulfilled life. Our music, our greeting cards, our ads on television, the pictures in our magazines all highlight "precious moments" shared with others. We tell the newly retired or the recently widowed, "Get involved. Keep busy." Perhaps nowhere is the relationship-centered ethos of our culture more clearly seen than in the proliferation of "family" businesses, based apparently upon the assumption that "family" sells. A quick check of my local suburban phone book reveals almost a full column of "family" businesses, including such unlikely combinations as a "family" meat market. In this manner marketers draw upon the relationship-oriented ethos of our society for the sake of profit.

The second irony is that the profession in which I have served for the past twenty-five years is itself highly focused on the importance of community and fellowship, subtly discouraging the idea of solitary self-renewal. How much of my time and energy as a parish priest has been spent in organizing activities and starting new groups so that people could feel "involved"? The fact is, the institutional church is highly extroverted. Church teaching, preaching, and programs are intended to engage the larger society and bring individuals into the community and fellowship of the church. Often, however, I have an uncomfortable feeling that the inner life of the spirit is largely ignored. The attitude of many in the church was expressed by a minister interviewed in the *MacNeil Report* who said, "Inward contemplation is selfish and the good Christian is *always* community centered."

THE WILDERNESS EXPERIENCE

This attitude has not always prevailed in the Judeo-Christian tradition as a whole. Until relatively recently, both solitude *and* community were perceived as two aspects of the spiritual path—contrasting, to be sure, but each nevertheless necessary in its own way. The history of Israel begins with Abraham, who is called to leave his community and pursue a solitary path in the wilderness:

> Go from your country and your kindred and your father's house to the land that I will show you. I will make of you a great nation, and I will bless you. (Genesis 12:1-2)

Later, when Abraham and Sarah's maid, Hagar, is alone in the wilderness, the Lord appears to her and confronts her with a most self-reflective question: "Hagar, slave-girl of Sarai, where have you come from and where are you going?" (Genesis 16:8). Similarly, Abraham's great-grandson, Joseph, encounters a mysterious stranger in the wilderness who asks, "What are you seeking?" (Genesis 37:15). It is in the wilderness that Jesus struggles with the tempter, just as, later, Paul also flees to the wilderness following his Damascus road experience (Galatians 1:17).

Throughout scripture, the wilderness functions in two ways: as an actual place where specific events occur and as a metaphor for solitude. Thus it is in the wilderness that we encounter God as well as the tempter, and where we are confronted with the basic questions of meaning and life mission. It is in the wilderness that we struggle with our sense of self-identity and where we finally gain a sense of personal clarity. And it is in the wilderness that we discover God to be not only present but present in a very personal way. Indeed, what we can claim for the wilderness in scripture—its dangers and opportunities—we can also claim for the role of solitude in our own personal life.

The Christian church also has a tradition of solitaries: in the fourth and fifth centuries numbers of Christians withdrew from the cities of the Roman Empire to live in solitary contemplation in the desert of the Nile Valley. The most notable of these Christians was St. Anthony, who lived in total seclusion for twenty years before forming a community of hermits in the desert. So pervasive was his influence that, within forty years of his death, the population of desert dwellers almost equaled that of the towns, although certainly not all of them were hermits.

Several centuries later the tradition of solitude reappeared in Celtic Christianity. Even today in England and Wales, there are as many as five hundred place-names, *disserth* or *dysart,* that recall the claiming of this desert of the heart. During the Middle Ages, those who felt called to a life in which solitude played a large role joined the great monastic communities. Even the word "monasticism" comes from the Greek word *monos,* meaning "alone." Especially during the late Middle Ages, the boundaries between monastic and secular life were less defined than they are today. Young girls could be remanded to a convent by fathers in order to avoid paying a dowry, and friends and relatives could live in the convent for extended periods as boarders.

Thus, the monastic life was accessible to the larger society in a way that is not true today, when probably not one person in a hundred personally knows someone living in a religious order.

Many other religions and cultures have valued solitude as a means for healing and for gaining knowledge of oneself. An example is the vision quest, practiced by Native Americans of the western plains. A young man, age twelve to sixteen, would spend two to five days in the wilderness seeking a dream or vision that would guide him in seeking his life path. A similar custom was the walkabout, practiced by the native tribes of Australia and New Zealand, in which a young person lived apart from the tribe for as long as a year while discovering his life mission. The vision quest and the walkabout are both rooted in a powerful affirmation of the efficacy of solitude in achieving self-insight.

According to Hindu belief, the individual progresses through a series of life stages, culminating in the hermit stage, during which the person's task is to withdraw from society and prepare for death. Although not literally practiced by most Hindu believers today, nevertheless this custom and the belief behind it is a strong affirmation of the need for solitary contemplation during the second half of life, an awareness that is almost entirely missing in our own society.

THE LOSS OF SOLITUDE

The curious phenomenon known as the Mojave phone booth is a sign of the loss of solitude in our culture. This isolated phone booth, located fourteen miles from the nearest paved road near the California-Nevada border in the Mojave Desert, receives dozens of calls a day from people all over the world—a housewife from New Zealand, a German high school student, a Seattle stockbroker. Individuals even make solitary pilgrimages to visit this legendary phone booth, which has several web-sites dedicated to it. The phenomenon started two years ago when a high-desert wanderer noticed a telephone icon on a Mojave Road Map. Curious, he tracked it to its source—a dilapidated phone booth fourteen miles down a treacherous dirt road accessible only by four-wheel-drive vehicles, installed by the phone company in the 1960s.

Why would people from all around the world call a number that no one will answer, and even make a personal visit to a phone booth located in the middle of the desert? The phenomenon of the Mojave phone booth speaks to our need to "reach out"—not to another person, but to the silence and solitude of the desert inside each of us. As people dial the number and then sit in their quiet apartment or their noisy office, hearing the phone ringing, I am sure they are transported, if only in their imaginations, to the silence and the solitude of the desert, where the sound of their call echoes on the silent rocks and sands. The wilderness, the desert and its silence and solitude, call to us, even today.

In less than a century we have moved from a pre-dominately rural to a predominately urban society. In previous generations, a majority of Americans lived in rural areas or in towns and villages within easy reach of rural areas. In contrast, since World

War II, Americans increasingly live in urban or semi-urban environments, continually surrounded by crowds of strangers. With the expansion of the modern metropolis, Americans can live forty or fifty miles from a major city in "cluster housing" and have as little space—physical and psychological—as if they were living in the city itself.

With the advent of pagers, cell phones, fax machines, and e-mail, moreover, we are all more connected and accessible than we were only a few years ago. We may be literally alone, as when we sit in front of our computer or when our cell phone is momentarily silenced, but do we experience the same *quality* of solitude now, when the outside world continually threatens to break in? Modern technology has reversed the nature of the relationship between the individual and the community. The monk in the Middle Ages was alone even in the midst of community; moderns are not truly alone even in our solitude.

Another important factor in the loss of solitude today is overcommitment. Whether or not Americans are in fact working longer hours than they were a generation ago, they *believe* themselves to have less time than ever before, and for many, leisure *feels* like work. Hours off the job are now spent taxiing children to highly structured and organized recreational activities, working out at crowded fitness clubs, or talking on the Internet. The result is that not only are parents and children *busier* than they were a generation ago, they are also more constantly *with* others.

The most important factor mitigating against solitude, however, is not environmental but ideological.
It is that we no longer *believe* in the beneficial effects
of solitude. We no longer perceive solitude as a
means to self-renewal and personal healing. The root
of this attitude may be found in the writings of
Sigmund Freud, who viewed the ability to form successful relationships as the key to emotional health
and personal fulfillment.

Anthony Storr, in his book *Solitude: A Return to
the Self*, summarizes the effects of Freudian thinking
on the psychological community and on the wider
society:

> The majority of psycho-analysts, social workers,
> and other members of the so-called helping pro-
> fessions consider that intimate personal relation-
> ships are the chief source of human happiness.
> Conversely, it is widely assumed that those who
> do not enjoy the satisfactions provided by such
> relationships are neurotic, immature, or in some
> other way abnormal.[2]

Society's attitude toward solitude was brought
home to me one day during the summer of eighth
grade. During my two weeks of camp, I would return
periodically to the campground for some quiet time
alone. One day the counselor discovered me away
from the other campers and expressed his concern:
Was I all right? Was I homesick? Was there some
problem between me and the other kids? I assured
him that I was fine and really preferred some time
alone. To his credit, he was able to accept this and
did not pressure me to rejoin the other children. The

incident, however, taught me an indelible lesson: solitude is not entirely acceptable, or at least is not considered a customary activity; we must be prepared to defend it at all times.

If true solitude is becoming harder to come by, have we lost anything of value? Are there gifts of solitude which we, as individuals and as a society, are poorer for not having received?

THE GIFTS OF SOLITUDE

One of the gifts of solitude, and one of the first to be discovered, is the gift of attentiveness, the ability to see the world with focus and intensity. Author Doris Grumbach writes of her experience during fifty days of solitude on the coast of Maine:

> Alone, I discovered myself looking hard at things, as if I were seeing them for the first time.... the shape of snow around the bird feeder where the feet of birds have tramped a wide circle in their search for fallen bird seed, the lovely V-shaped wake of a family of newly arrived eider ducks as they cross the cove, the sight of a green log sputtering and drooling sap in the woodstove.[3]

Solitude promises to renew in us that sense of really *seeing* things, really *noticing* things. How different this is from the way most of us spend our days, constantly rushing from one thing to another, "getting things done." One columnist suggested that a symbol of the contemporary person is the man or woman standing in front of the microwave as it ticks off the seconds, muttering, "Come on! Come on!" In

the litany for Ash Wednesday, Episcopalians ask
God's forgiveness for "the impatience of our lives."[4]
Periodic times of solitude help slow us down and get
us back in touch with God's rhythm of life.

Related to the gift of attentiveness is the gift of
healing. Injured animals instinctively steal away to a
hidden spot. So also do injured humans, whether
that injury is spiritual, emotional, or physical. No
one would deny that people play a crucial role in
healing. But there is an aspect of spiritual and emotional healing that seems best accomplished alone,
especially when that healing relates to coming to
terms with loss or with some significant change in
one's life. This dimension is reflected in the gospel
accounts of Jesus' journey into the wilderness; both
Matthew and Luke say that Jesus was "led" by the
Spirit into the wilderness, while Mark states that the
Spirit "drove" him. I suspect that Mark's more vis-
ceral language is a better reflection of Jesus' emotional state. When we experience profound
life-changing circumstances, our need for solitude is
often a compulsion.

Personal clarity, insight, and creativity are other
gifts of solitude. The writer, the artist, the musical
composer, even the developer of computer software
are professionals who spend much of their time
working alone. But others in more sociable professions draw on periods of solitude for many of their
most creative ideas. As a priest I find my best sermons emerge from walks in the woods or time on
vacation. Furthermore, solitude often reveals interests we did not know we had. One day, on a whim,
a college professor picks up his woodworking tools,

neglected for many years, and rediscovers the pleasure of crafting something with his hands. A passion reborn in solitude, woodworking becomes a way of incorporating solitude into his life. Solitude thus provides fertile ground for expressing the interests we know we have and for discovering entirely new interests.

The greatest gift of solitude, however, is an awareness of the presence of God. God is often discovered in a very *personal* way during periods of solitude. It is interesting that God was never present to the chosen people quite so much as he was during their wilderness journey. Similarly, the great religious leaders—Jesus, Buddha, Mohammed—typically withdrew into solitude before emerging to share their insight with the world. Indeed, scripture often affirms a link between silence, solitude, and the presence of God: "Be still," the Lord tells the psalmist, "and know that I am God!" (Psalm 46:10). Although Christians typically celebrate the presence of God in a communal celebration of the eucharist, those celebrations, for many of the individuals gathered together, commemorate and reflect personal life-changing events that originally occurred in solitude.

If solitude in fact leads us toward attentiveness, personal healing, insight, clarity, and an experience of the presence of God, then we would expect many individuals to be hungry for the gifts of solitude in our own day. And indeed this appears to be the case.

A HUNGER FOR SOLITUDE
We can see this hunger for solitude clearly in a significant change in our language. The phrase "I need

my own space" has now become a commonplace. This use of the word "space" to denote a kind of personal psychological enclave has an interesting and revealing history. It first appeared in the language in the mid 1300s and remained in common usage for three hundred years until the mid 1600s, when it disappeared. As recently as 1983, the ninth edition of *Webster's New Collegiate Dictionary* listed ten definitions of space, none of them denoting the psychological dimension. However, in the tenth edition, a new definition of space was added: "The opportunity to assert or experience one's identity or needs freely." Why would a particular definition of a word, obsolete for three centuries, suddenly reappear in the language? The answer is obvious: because the concept embodied by that usage has once again become relevant to large numbers of people. It is in the concept of "needing one's own space" that we find an inchoate and unconscious longing for solitude.

Why is this renewal of interest in solitude occurring? What is it people are hungering for when they say they "want their own space" or when they go on retreat? On the simplest and most basic level it may well be a desire to escape, even if only momentarily, the unrelenting busyness of their lives. On a deeper level—and often unrecognized even by the individuals themselves—the hunger for solitude appears to be a hunger for the *gifts* of solitude: for spiritual and emotional healing, for regaining a sense of meaning and purpose, and for getting back in touch with ultimate realities. In this sense the hunger for solitude is nothing less than a search for God.

A PERSONAL NOTE

In this book it is my premise that occasional periods of solitude are a need for all of us. This need may well be as basic as the opposite and contrasting need for attachment, for relationship. In solitude our souls, minds, and bodies are nurtured in ways that only come about when we are alone. As a society and as individuals, we need to regain a healthy balance between solitude and involvement, withdrawal and engagement. Almost a generation ago, Anne Morrow Lindbergh stated the dilemma for all of us when she wrote:

> The solution for me, surely, is neither in total renunciation of the world, nor in total accept-ance of it. I must find a balance somewhere, or an alternating rhythm between these two extremes; a swinging of the pendulum between solitude and communion, between retreat and return. In my periods of retreat, perhaps I can learn something to carry back into my worldly life.[5]

In a normal, healthy state we would move back and forth between periods of solitude and periods of engagement. But when involvement *alone* is valued by a society, when the periodic need for solitude is unrecognized or ignored, the result is that we become increasingly exhausted, depleted, and in need of this most basic means of spiritual and emotional renewal.

Solitude, however, needs to be perceived as more than a way to recharge our batteries so that we can return to the same assumptions and the same lifestyle that have brought us to the point of exhaustion and depletion in the first place. The practice of solitude presents an opportunity to challenge these very assumptions and lifestyle issues. Thus, in the largest sense, solitude is a path of repentance, of "turning again" on the way to embracing a healthier and more balanced life expression that is aware of the presence of God.

In this book I will discuss the gifts of solitude, including healing and gaining a sense of personal clarity and mission, that are part of experiencing God. I also discuss the dark side of solitude—why we fear solitude and how, and whether our fears are justified. More than presenting an objective treatment of solitude, I argue in *favor* of it, as one antidote to the mindless busyness and over-engagement of contemporary life. I use images and stories from scripture as a point of departure to discuss solitude. I also draw upon my own experiences when they seem relevant.

During the writing of this book I have become increasingly aware—and accepting of—my own need for solitude. I have found myself strongly identifying with the contemporary writer who remarked: "From the start, I knew this time was essential, but I did not realize to what degree. I found that sex, hunger, and thirst were subordinate to my quest for solitude."[6] Writing this book has given me permission to reclaim my own solitude and its gifts. In the Sermon on the Mount Jesus tells us that "blessed are those who hunger and thirst for righteousness" (Matthew 5:6). In our more secular age, we do not typically speak of hungering and thirsting for "righteousness." We speak instead in such self-centered terms as "needing my own space." But even in our reductive language, there is a quality of hungering and thirsting for something deeper, something we cannot put into words, but that we intuitively sense is real and genuine and life-giving. We know, onsome level, that solitude is, indeed, a neglected path to God.

QUESTIONS FOR REFLECTION

1. Have you had an experience of solitude that changed your life? What were the circumstances? How did it change you?

2. Are you aware of a desire to experience more solitude in your own life, or are the ways you currently experience solitude sufficient to address your need? How does a need for solitude manifest itself in your life?

3. In what ways you do find that our culture discourages individuals from being alone? How do you see a hunger for solitude reflected in the larger society and in the lives of the people you know?

4. Some of the gifts of solitude include greater attentiveness to one's surroundings, insight, clarity, and an awareness of the presence of God. Have you experienced any of these gifts during periods of solitude? What other gifts have you experienced? How have you integrated them into your life?

CHAPTER TWO

The Dangers of Solitude

In the last chapter I spoke of the gifts of solitude and of the hunger many people have to rediscover these gifts in their own lives. But there is also a side of solitude that we fear: being alone. And unless we can name this fear and decide for ourselves whether it is justified, we will be unlikely to claim the solitude we need and to receive the gifts it can give us.

The potential loneliness of solitude was brought home to me during a conversation with a church member. I was at that time feeling very "evangelical" about solitude and I had preached an impassioned sermon on its benefits. After church a woman in her eighties came up to me and said quietly, "You know, Chris, solitude can be dangerous, especially for the elderly." As she was saying this I pictured her husband, once a busy professional but now largely confined to his own home. I thought also of other shut-in members of the church I visited on a regular basis. One woman in particular came to mind whose entire world consisted of the four walls of her small apartment, her routine broken occasionally by trips to the doctor or visits from members of her family. Yes, indeed, solitude can be a problem for the elderly, I thought to myself.

Shortly after this conversation I received a phone call from another church member. She was worried about her sister, a teacher in her forties and the single mother of a four year old. Her sister was desperately lonely and in need of connecting with other people, but her whole life was work and childcare. During a recent illness she had felt very vulnerable and disconnected. Who would take her four year old to preschool, should she become incapacitated? In fact, who would take care of *her*? Clearly, we can be outwardly busy and involved in the world and nevertheless inwardly feel disconnected and lonely.

About a year later the dark side of solitude was brought home to me in a very personal way. In connection with writing this book I had made arrangements to stay alone in a house in Maine for a week in January. I was looking forward to this time of getting up when I wanted, going to bed when I wanted. Mornings I would spend working at my desk looking out on the ocean. Afternoons I would walk on the golf course or along the beach with the dog. After that, back to the house for a glass of wine, a quiet dinner, a video, and then bed.

As the time for my week came nearer, I became increasingly aware that I would be, indeed, completely alone—and with the summer residents gone, alone for a radius of several houses around. I found myself thinking about that moment when I would turn out the light and get into bed and the darkness would gather around me. When I had first seen this house in August, I had noticed a tiny graveyard outside the front door—six graves of sailors lost in a shipwreck a century and a half before. The graveyard had seemed so charming when I saw it in August, with the yellow of the daisies contrasting against the gray stones. Would this graveyard be equally charming fifty feet away from the front door on a dark night in January?

The fact was, it was not a fear of flesh and blood I was experiencing. It was a fear of something else. I found myself embarrassed—here I was, a responsible fifty-six-year-old Episcopal priest with a wife and two teenaged children, and I was afraid of ghosts and "things that go bump in the night." Furthermore, in addition to these "irrational" fears, I had some social concerns in connection with this time alone. Would I become, even to a small degree, strange or "odd" during that week alone in Maine? Would I begin to lose my ability to relate easily to people? Would I perhaps discover that I liked solitude all too well?

Where do these and other fears regarding solitude come from? Why is it that even those drawn to solitude, such as myself, also fear it? Above all, are we *right* to fear solitude? *Are* there dangers of which we should be aware? These are important questions because, as I said at the beginning of this chapter, unless we come to terms with our fear of solitude, we will be unlikely to claim its gifts.

THE FEAR OF SOLITUDE

Ester Schaler Buchholz suggests in her book *The Call of Solitude* that our fear of solitude may be rooted in childhood fears of abandonment and neglect: as infants we cannot provide for ourselves the basic needs for food, warmth, or relief from distress. In childhood, we may also be frightened of solitude because of its use as a punishment: "If you are not good you will be sent to your room." Solitude therefore becomes undesired and undesirable. In addition, as we grow to maturity we encounter society's negative attitude toward solitude and toward those who seek it out. Buchholz writes: "Invariably, alonetime meets with social questioning if not censure.... People associate going it alone with unnecessary risk taking and antisocial pursuits."[1]

Fear of boredom may be another reason for a dread of solitude. Our society provides us little encouragement to be alone, and therefore few resources. It is not surprising that many people find solitude boring. The problem, of course, is not solitude; it is the lack of inner resources to deal creatively with it and to achieve a "good solitude."

Finally, fear of death may contribute to our fear of solitude. On some unconscious level we fear that time when we will be *ultimately* alone, *ultimately* solitary. Faith tells us that we will be part of a community, the "communion of saints." But such assurances do not entirely assuage our fear of death and therefore, by extension, our fear of solitude.

Our fear, then, comes from many sources. As a result, most of us are at best ambiguous about solitude—we fear it even while we are attracted to it. Interestingly enough, the Bible is also ambiguous about solitude and in fact reflects our own contemporary ambivalence toward it rather well. On the one hand, the gospels repeatedly relate how Jesus retreated to a "lonely place" to pray. Furthermore, what Jesus experienced in these lonely places was apparently sufficiently compelling to the disciples that they wanted to experience the fruits of the same: "Lord, teach us to pray." We read also in scripture of individuals, such as the prophet Elijah, who experienced self-renewal and a regained sense of personal mission as a result of a period of solitude.

On the other hand, solitude is often equated with "the wilderness" in scripture—a place of danger. It is in the wilderness that Jesus meets the tempter. It is there, too, that Jacob wrestles with a mysterious antagonist—an encounter rooted perhaps in the ancient belief in *jinn*, or demonic spirits, of the desert tradition. For the Israelites, life was lived in community; therefore one of the worst punishments was to be sent alone into exile, as was Cain after the murder of Abel. When we encounter solitary individuals in scripture, their solitude is seldom the result of choice: perhaps they have been expelled from their household, like Hagar and her child, or were pursuing a solitary task, as Moses or David were when tending sheep. Even in the Wisdom books, the "self-help" literature of its day, we read in vain for admonitions to renew ourselves by getting away and claiming some "space" as we would today.

Scripture clearly reflects our own ambivalence about solitude and recognizes its dangers, but at the same time it also affirms the potential of solitude. The wilderness may be a place of danger, but it is also a place for transformation: for regaining personal clarity, a sense of one's own life mission, and closeness with God.

SOLITUDE AND LONELINESS

The fact is, we cannot discuss the difficulties of solitude without differentiating between solitude and loneliness. Indeed, it is *loneliness,* and the fear of loneliness, that prevents many people from experiencing a "good solitude." What is the difference between solitude and loneliness? British psychiatrist Anthony Storr, drawing on experiences of prisoners held in solitary confinement, suggests that *involuntary* experiences of solitude are experienced negatively and therefore produce negative consequences.[2] Storr's observations allow us to draw an important distinction between solitude and loneliness. Solitude is *chosen*; it is a state that we willingly enter into, for the purpose of self-renewal, personal clarity, or some other reason. Loneliness, on the other hand, is *involuntary*; it happens *to* us. In fact, what makes loneliness so devastating is precisely the fact that lonely people can see no way out, either because of self-perceived circumstances that keep them in a state of loneliness (demanding work schedules, childcare responsibilities, lack of opportunities to meet new people) or because of temperamental characteristics that prevent them from relating effectively to others (shyness, embarrassment, or even, in extreme cases, social phobia). Unlike Anthony Storr's prisoners held in solitary confinement, they are not literally prisoners. However, like them, their solitude is perceived as involuntary, and therefore is experienced negatively as loneliness. *The Book of Common Prayer* distinguishes well between loneliness and solitude in the prayer "For Those Who Live Alone," in which we pray that such individuals "may not be lonely in their solitude" (BCP 829).

Loneliness, however, is a complex emotion. It is not necessarily alleviated simply by the physical presence of others. Indeed, loneliness can be caused by an internal emptiness, as sociologist David Reisman pointed out forty years ago in his seminal work *The Lonely Crowd: A Study of the Changing American Character.* Since many Americans seek personal meaning and a sense of self-affirmation only outside themselves, they would tend to feel lonely even in a "crowd." Nor should we assume that solitude and the experience of community are mutually exclusive. It may well be that involvement in a community provides the very sense of spiritual and emotional well-being that makes it possible to achieve a "good solitude." Psychologist Mary Piper, author of *Reviving Ophelia,* described in a recent newspaper article a reality that is true of many Americans: "We have gone from community and solitude to crowds and loneliness."

It is ironic that while many of us are feeling solitude deprived, many others are increasingly lonely. In 1995 Robert Putnam, a Harvard professor, pub-

lished an article entitled "Bowling Alone," in which
he pointed to a curious phenomenon. While the total
number of bowlers in America had increased by ten
percent between 1980 and 1993, league bowling—
that is, the number who bowl as members of organized leagues—had plummeted by forty percent.
Putnam noted similarly declining patterns of mem-
bership in such organizations as churches, the PTA,
the Red Cross, and the Boy Scouts. More and more
Americans seem to be "bowling alone" in various
areas of their lives, and the consequences for large
numbers of people are loneliness, isolation, and disengagement.[3]

Perhaps for this very reason, solitude is arguably
of greater danger to us today than it was in previous
generations because we have no tradition of the creative use of solitude to draw upon. The desert fathers
of the third and fourth centuries developed a sophis-
ticated theological and psychological understanding
of solitude and its uses. Similarly, the monks of the
Middle Ages ordered their lives around a "rule"
developed by St. Benedict and others that incorporated formal periods of solitude into the context of
life in community. Such monastic rules as St.
Benedict's were, for the most part, based upon an
intuitive understanding of the needs of individuals
and of human psychology in general. Unlike such
previous eras, we possess no such philosophical
understanding of the purpose of solitude and no
"technology" for achieving it. No wonder so many
fall into loneliness.

DEPRESSION, ISOLATION,
AND ILLUSION

In addition to loneliness, another manifestation of the dark side of solitude is that of depression, especially as the result of traumatic events such as the death of a spouse, a serious illness, or the loss of a job. For those with a preexisting tendency toward depression or despondency, solitude may draw it out. Writer Doris Grumbach recounts such an experience in her memoir, *Fifty Days of Solitude*. During the hard winter of 1993, Grumbach took advantage of an opportunity to spend some concentrated time alone. She retreated to her cottage on the northern coast of Maine, where her nearest neighbors were two or three acres away, shielded from view by a wall of trees. Whole days passed without talking to another person. Grumbach's intention during this period was to indulge her natural penchant for solitude but also to explore her inner life, to discover, as she writes, "if something was still living in there." She spent her days performing simple household chores, listening to music, reading, and observing life on the cove. She befriended a solitary winter housefly, homebound like herself, and writes of a newfound ability to see inanimate things as "new objects, seen in a curious, hard original light, no longer ordinary or familiar."[4]

But Grumbach also reflects on another side of her experience. Earlier she had noted that, throughout her life, .friends had remarked that her mind was too "Gothic," that her mental life was lived in dark medieval towers and dungeons. In the past she had been able to bury, or at least temporarily forget, a tendency toward despondency. Now, however, alone in her cottage, she writes: "Solitude becomes the rich breeding ground for my natural depression.... Without company I have had to remember that despair is always lurking beyond the circle of lamplight."[5] In spite of this tendency toward depression, Grumbach is able to find solace in solitude. Toward the end of her fifty days she writes:

> If I have learned anything in these days, it is that the proper conditions for productive solitude are old age and the outside presence of a small portion of the beauty of the world. Given these, and the drive to explore and understand an inner territory, solitude can be an enlivening, even exhilarating experience.[6]

The desert fathers spoke of the "demon of dejection," which St. John of the Cross described as "a thick and heavy cloud...upon the soul." In solitude, especially if following some traumatic event, there is always the danger that an individual may become stuck in depression. When this occurs, admonitions to "Get busy, get involved," are not only well intentioned; they are also wise. The fact is, depression can masquerade as a desire for solitude and it is not always easy to recognize the difference, especially when it involves yourself. A friend once remarked to me that, after her husband's death, all she wanted was to be alone, a desire she communicated to all her friends. It was only subsequently that she recognized this desire for solitude for what it was—simply a manifestation of depression following the death of her husband.

Related to the danger of depression is the danger of isolation. A friend of mine writes, "Isolation is my natural state. It is my 'center of gravity.' It is the state to which I naturally return unless I take steps to struggle against it." Introverts possess a natural gift for solitude but they also possess a tendency toward isolation.

An opposite and contrasting danger of solitude is inflation of the ego, which leads to a sense of unreality, or what the Christian tradition has called pride or vainglory. These are all manifestations of what the mystics called "illusion." This danger is hinted at in the temptation story, when the tempter shows Jesus "all the kingdoms of the world" and promises him, "To you I will give their glory and all this authority" (Luke 4:5, 6). In a very different context the danger of ego inflation as a result of excessive solitude is well illustrated by unibomber Ted Kozinski in his mountain cabin, composing a thirty-thousand-word manifesto for *The New York Times*. In less extreme forms, inflation may manifest itself simply as eccentricity. Reflecting on her experience as a solitary, Doris Grumbach writes, "The beasts in the solitary jungle through which I have continued to walk are spiritual oddity and growing eccentricity."[7]

Solitude, then, does indeed have its dangers, consisting of loneliness, depression, isolation, self-inflation, and eccentricity. It is important to remember, however, that the journey into the self, which those drawn to solitude are often called upon to make, usually involves some degree of pain and suffering. A famous story is told of the friends of St. Anthony, who stood outside the door of his cell appalled at the

shrieks and groans emanating from within as
Anthony wrestled with his demons in solitude. The
idea that pain and suffering can be avoided, that they
are not rather a means to the eventual healing of the
personality, would have been an alien concept up to
modern times. Priest and psychologist John Sanford
writes:

> The maturation of the ego . . . requires the break-
> ing down of the old eccentric ego. . . . In the lan-
> guage of the New Testament, this is what is
> meant by *metanoia*. . . . Such a process necessi-
> tates a good deal of suffering. It includes facing
> one's fears. . . . It is necessary that the individual
> face his shadow—his own dark, feared side—and
> pass through a time of personal darkness.[8]

During painful times of transition, it is important
to keep in mind the potential healing power of even
the most difficult solitude. It is true that Jesus
encountered the tempter in the wilderness. But it was
as a result of this encounter that Jesus clarified his
self-identity and the shape of his ministry. Similarly,
Jacob's antagonist in Genesis (32:22-32) reveals himself to be an angel of the Lord or perhaps even the
Lord himself. True, Jacob is wounded by the
encounter, but he wins for himself a blessing and a
new name.

Such was the experience of a thirty-year-old pedi-
atric nurse who left the comforts of home and routine in a wealthy Philadelphia suburb to serve as a
medical missionary in the Dominican Republic. Gail
remembers flying into Santo Domingo and being
confronted by the smell of burning garbage hanging

over the city. She remembers her first day being
bussed to the site of her first medical mission and
seeing two hundred people lined up as if waiting for
the bank to open. "What are these people waiting
for?" Gail asked. "They're waiting for you," was the
reply. She remembers treating children in advanced
stages of malnutrition, the result of easily treatable
medical conditions, such as a cleft lip or a cleft
palate. She remembers taking "sun showers"—water
heated in a pail—at the end of each day and sleeping
under mosquito netting in a compound patrolled by
armed guards. "Get me out of here," she phoned to
her parents at the end of the first couple of days.

Her moment of revelation occurred while alone
on a jungle trail. Gail had been reassessing the whole
course of her life, including a destructive relationship
in which she was caught. Suddenly the way became
clear to her. Gail believes her solitude and her
removal from the pressures of her own culture led
her to new insights. "I believe God puts you in such
a situation," she said later. "He strips you of all outside stimuli. All your ordinary concerns and worries
are removed and suddenly you can see clearly."
There is a price to be paid for this clarity, however.
Gail now sometimes feels herself to be out of step
with the typical concerns of many of her contempo-
raries. "I find myself confronting problems and situ-
ations in my own life and the lives of others and I
say, 'It really doesn't matter. There are people starv-
ing out there. This other really isn't that important.'"
There is a certain loneliness in this new-found perspective.

Gail finds that God is in the loneliness, however. "He gives you gifts in other ways," she remarks. "He gave me a sense of purpose. He gave me peace. I experienced the truth of that passage from scripture, the Lord will 'give unto them beauty for others, the oil of joy for mourning.' The trip had a domino effect on me. All the positive new directions in my life started with it. Before I left, a medical colleague said to me, 'You know, Gail, this isn't going to change your life. But it will make you feel better for a while.' When I returned, I said to him, 'You know what? You were wrong. It *did* change my life.'"

What her story shows is that, in spite of the danger of loneliness, for many people there may be no alternative to solitude in order to regain emotional and spiritual health. Inevitably, we will need to be alone when facing a major loss or coming to a radically changed perception of ourselves. Even if we are fortunate enough to have a supportive community, even a supportive *church* community, our deepest instincts at a time of crisis may well be to "go it alone" for some period of time. We remember that Jesus was led but also "driven" into the wilderness. For those who feel themselves similarly driven to come to terms with changed circumstances in their own lives, it may subsequently be said of them, as it was said of Moses by an early Christian biographer, Gregory of Nyssa, that he "entered the darkness, and then found God in it."

SAFEGUARDS

What safeguards do we have against the dangerous aspects of solitude? How can we seek the gifts of solitude without the danger of falling into its dark side?

First, if we are serious about incorporating a greater degree of solitude into our spiritual life, we should give thought to seeking out a spiritual director. We will look in more detail at the role of a spiritual director in chapter eight. For now, suffice it to say that either a formal spiritual director or an informal "soul friend" may be of great help in combating the potential dangers of solitude.

Another safeguard is to be a member of a supportive community. This may be a formal support group convened for that very purpose, or it may be a loose affiliation of friends and family who care about you. Individuals already involved in prayer or Bible study groups, book groups, parenting groups, twelve-step programs, or colleague support groups already have a potential community to fall back upon. Whether your support group is formally or informally constituted, it should be one that encourages your spiritual and emotional growth and your desire to incorporate a greater degree of solitude into your life.

Thirdly, a safe way to experience periods of solitude is to go on a retreat. Conducted in religious houses or retreat centers and led by experienced religious or lay leaders, such retreats may last for a day, a weekend, three or four days, or for longer periods. A typical format is for the leader to give meditations on a selected topic and then provide ample time to pray, reflect, sit quietly, or walk about the grounds of the retreat center. One advantage of such retreats, which have become increasingly popular in recent years, is that they enable you to slow down, to get back in touch with God and yourself, and to begin to incorporate the healing power of solitude into your life.

Probably the most important safeguard against the "demons" of solitude, however, is simply to maintain a normal life in the world. In his autobiography, psychologist Carl Jung wrote of the period in his late thirties when he explored the depths of his unconscious. During this time bizarre fantasies and images assaulted him. There were times when he feared he was going mad. Many years later, Jung wrote:

> Particularly at this time...I needed a point of support in "this world," and I may say my family and my professional work were that to me. It was most essential for me to have a normal life in the real world as a counterpoise to that strange inner world. My family and my profession remained the base to which I could always return.... I have a medical diploma from a Swiss university, I must help my patients, I have a wife and five children, I live at 228 Seestrasse in Kusnacht—these were actualities which made demands upon me and proved to me again and again that I really existed, that I was not a blank page whirling about in the winds of the spirit.... Thus my family and my profession always remained a joyful reality and a guarantee that I also had a normal existence.[9]

One fundamental question remains. If we recognize the potential dangers of solitude as well as the social pressures against those who seek it out, why should we pursue it at all? Chiefly for two reasons: first, because our nature requires it. The healthy human organism seems to require a balance between engagement and solitude, between inner and outer involvements. Second, because for most people and under most circumstances, the potential benefits of solitude far outweigh the potential dangers. Solitude provides not only needed relief from the busyness and over-engagement of our lives. It provides also the opportunity to discover—or to rediscover—who we are, who God is calling us to be.

This was indeed my experience during my week alone in Maine, which I described at the beginning of this chapter. What I had feared did not materialize: I did not become strange or "odd" away from my ordinary contacts with people. The darkness of the house at night did not gather around me when I turned out the lights and went to bed. Even the graveyard in the front yard remained a benign presence, the stones glistening under their cover of January snow. In fact my days passed pleasantly and even joyously, following my own self-appointed routine. I would work at my desk three or four hours every morning. Afternoons were for rest and relaxation. I would take long walks on the beach listening to the gulls. One afternoon I took the dog and went sledding on the golf course. The days followed one another in a fulfilling solitary routine of work and relaxation.

There was, however, one major surprise that I encountered during my week alone. It was my need for people. As much as I did not want to see people during the day, especially when I was working, I found I very much wanted to see them in the evening, when work was done. I discovered that, when I had a social engagement planned for the evening, the knowledge of this tended to focus and energize my day. On the other hand, when I had nothing planned, I found it was necessary to leave the house to go out to dinner or to a movie.

My week in Maine, then, provided both a confirmation and also a surprise. The confirmation was that my ordinary, day-to-day routine in the "real world" was not providing for me the solitude and the renewal I needed on a regular basis. This was no surprise. What *was* a surprise was that I, a relatively solitary person, apparently needed people to a greater degree than I had realized. I did not know whether to be pleased or a little put off. I had always prided myself on being self-sufficient. And now I was focusing my day on whether or not I had a dinner invitation! Nevertheless, the insight that I needed *both* people *and* solitude came as a kind of healing revelation, a topic we will discuss more fully in the next chapter.

QUESTIONS FOR REFLECTION

1. How would you describe your own attitude toward solitude? Do you tend to resist it or to welcome opportunities for it? What circumstances in your own past have contributed to your attitude?

2. Moore distinguishes between solitude and loneliness. Think back to times of each in your life. How would you describe the difference between solitude and loneliness? Does the fear of loneliness discourage you from seeking solitude?

3. Sometimes solitude can be the best means for working through a personal crisis. Recollect such a time of crisis in your life. What part, if any, did solitude play?

4. Which potential dangers of solitude have you personally experienced? What safeguards have you found effective?

CHAPTER THREE

The Healing Power of Solitude

It was really the rock that brought it home to her. It was a large oblong rock—"curvilinear," they would have called it back in her art school days—on the edge of the beach in this seaside town on the Outer Banks of North Carolina. She had really *looked* at it. She had really *noticed* it. She had wandered down from the cottage with a cup of tea in her hands, sat on an adjoining rock, and studied it for more than an hour. An hour! How long had it been since she had given something such attention? How long had it been since she had given attention to something that was really *hers*, something that related to *her* interests, *her* gifts, *her* abilities?

Sitting on her rock, sipping the last of the tea in the warm November sunlight, she ran her eyes along the incised lines of the stone where the water and tides had written their pattern on its surface. She could not help but reflect on the endurance of this rock, buffeted by winds and waves for thousands of years while still maintaining the integrity of its shape and even developing its own unique beauty, shaped by the very elements that buffeted it. If this rock could endure, so perhaps could she.

Her presence on the beach was the result of a long period of emotional turmoil. For some time she had been experiencing an intense desire to get away, to remove herself from her ordinary surroundings. This desire had become something of a compulsion. She had thought from time to time of Mark's description of Jesus as being "driven" into the wilderness, and she had felt herself no less driven by inner forces she did not understand. Accordingly she had closed up her house in the city, told the few necessary people that she would be away, and given herself this weekend alone in the cottage by the sea, this place that had been a "home away from home" for her family for the past two decades.

That weekend, as she walked mile after mile upon the beach listening to the cries of the gulls, as she returned to the cottage several times a day for a cup of tea, as she accomplished her few household tasks with a care and attention and awareness that she had not directed toward anything in years, she began to feel something that she had not felt in months: the beginning of a sense of peace. The words of one of the psalms came back to her:

> I have calmed and quieted my soul
> like a child quieted at its mother's breast;
> like a child that is quieted is my soul.
> (Psalm 131:2, RSV)

What a marvelous image of God this was, she thought—God as a mother gathering a child to her breast.

As she reflected on these words, she was surprised to realize that God was not specifically identified as the nurturer. "*I* have calmed and quieted my soul," wrote the psalmist. Apparently the psalmist had done some self-nurturing, some "self-care." She realized that part of what she was doing this weekend was in the category of self-nurturing. But what surprised her was that she seemed to be experiencing something that went beyond self-nurturing. The fact was, when she gave herself this weekend she had not been aware that she was looking for God, much less seeking specifically "religious" answers to the issues in her life. Nevertheless, as the quiet hours succeeded one another, she became aware of a Presence. She felt herself being fed by a source of strength and comfort that was not of her own origin. She found herself experiencing what she had not experienced for a long time, the beginnings of "the peace of God, which surpasses all understanding" (Philippians 4:7). When she had heard these words in the past, she had often found herself wondering what exactly that peace was and what it felt like to experience it. Now she was beginning to know. It was a growing sense of acceptance of the changes in her life, an acceptance of herself as the person she was before and as the person she was now, and, above all, an acceptance of

God as the ultimate source of nurturing in her life. The peace that she was feeling did indeed "surpass all understanding." She could not "explain" it. It could only be experienced. It simply *was*.

Silence was a large part of that weekend. The first morning in the cottage she had turned on the radio but she soon found the cheery chatter of the radio talk show host to be an intrusion. She preferred instead to listen to other sounds—the creaking of the floor boards as she walked to the kitchen, the wind whistling around the porch outside—and even the sound of the silence itself. Above all, she wanted to hear the sound of her own thoughts. How long had it been, she wondered, since she had really *listened*?

She wondered if she was practicing what the mystics call "attentiveness." In any case, she found herself cherishing the silence, silence which, in the past and under other circumstances, had often seemed oppressive. "For God alone my soul waits in silence," the psalmist had written (62:1). Indeed, it was *in* the silence that she found herself experiencing a sense of the presence of God. It was in the silence that she felt her self-nurturing being transformed into something deeper, whose source was beyond her own self.

That weekend she sensed something new—a growing sense of resolution; a feeling of wanting to get on with her life; a desire to be like that rock, buffeted by the wind and waves but nevertheless enduring, with her own unique, strong beauty shaped by the very forces that had buffeted her. The healing really started that weekend. She discovered a truth about herself that became more and more evident in the weeks ahead, that there was a "me" that existed apart from her relations with others, that not only *was* there a "me," but that the "me" was loved and cherished and nurtured in ways that she could not even begin to comprehend. And later that spring, when she took the first tentative steps back to her art after twenty years, again experiencing the feel of clay between her fingers, and even began to fashion an art studio for herself, she was not entirely surprised at the strength of her resolution, because it had started that weekend six months before. It had started with the rock, the silence, and the solitude.

THE CIRCLES OF HEALING

These recollections are those of a woman at mid-life dealing with major changes in her life. But they could also describe the experience of a middle-aged man coping with divorce, separation, or the loss of a job, an older person dealing with the death of a loved one, a young adult coming to terms with the end of a relationship, or an adolescent mourning the end of childhood. The fact is, all human beings experience pain and loss, growth and transformation, and finally healing and wholeness. These are archetypal experiences and, by their very nature, are often mediated most intensely in solitude.

The healing we typically experience in solitude is first a healing of ourselves. Most of us live lives that are significantly out of balance. We routinely ignore our needs for renewal of mind, body, and spirit. We have lost touch with any inner sense of vocation or call, and consequently our lives seem to lack meaning and purpose. Many of us are pathologically busy.

In addition, when we do crave solitude, it is often in response to a life crisis or major life transition. Instinctively we sense that the healing we seek is likely to be found in solitude, away from the demands and distractions of our ordinary routine. Consequently, the first circle of healing in solitude is a healing of ourselves.

The second circle is a healing of our relationships with others. It is ironic that we are brought back into closer relationship with others by the act of leaving them for a time, but such is often the case. In solitude we are able to gain greater perspective on our relationships. We are removed from the daily annoyances of living with others, and we may find our affections rekindled. We often return from a period alone freshly resolved to live out our relationships with more grace and patience. A healing of relationships is the second gift of solitude.

Finally, in solitude, we may find ourselves brought back into closer relationship with God. This may occur even when we are not anticipating it or especially looking for it. Anne Morrow Lindbergh once spoke of her intentions in seeking solitude: "I was not looking for God. I was looking for myself."[1] Nevertheless, whether sought or not, the presence of God is often experienced in our solitude. Being alone offers the potential to bring us back into right relationship with the Presence at the center of our being.

The healing that occurs in solitude then, is a healing that results from being brought back into right relationship with ourselves, with others, and with God. Solitude is, however, as the title of the book suggests, a *neglected* path to God. By this I mean we do not ordinarily seek out solitude, nor does our society easily give us "permission"—much less encouragement—to enter into it. Consequently, when we do experience solitude, it is often not because we have intentionally entered into it but rather because we have been *driven* into it, either by life circumstances or by emotional and spiritual forces beyond our control. In this chapter we explore the healing power of solitude, and will begin by identifying several common elements.

GETTING AWAY

A large part of the healing power of solitude is the simple act of getting away from one's ordinary surroundings—of removing oneself to a different physical and/or psychological space. At such moments we experience what we call a "sea change," but this sea change does not require long stretches of time: it can also occur during the course of a two-hour trip to the mountains or a five-minute walk in the woods. It is fascinating how often in scripture watershed events in the lives of individuals or whole peoples are marked by journeys, such as Moses to Midian or Paul to Arabia. The traditional Christian practice of making a pilgrimage to some holy spot is based in part upon the spiritually transforming power of removing oneself from familiar surroundings. Even the recently revived custom of walking the labyrinth has at its heart the concept of a journey. For many people even the commute to and from work is a time of reinvigorating solitude.

This act of removing oneself, of changing one's environment, need not necessarily involve traveling great distances or, indeed, any distance at all. For the Hindu living in a traditional Indian household, the journey may be no more than a walk across the room to the meditation area set off from the household by a simple curtain. For the Christian, it may be simply a short meditation on the psalms while performing household tasks. I myself have a custom of walking outside my house, usually at dawn, and standing for a few moments in silence as the day gathers about me. My "journey" is only fifty feet from the house to the street. And yet I find that this change of environment, as minimal as it is, along with the silence and mental focusing, helps prepare me for the day. Indeed for those practicing a solitude of the mind, which we will discuss later in this chapter, the journey is not physical but psychological and spiritual. In whatever manner a change of environment is accomplished, whether by traveling a great distance or no distance at all, the journey itself is the first step in the healing process.

Furthermore, the journey of which we speak is not necessarily voluntarily undertaken. In fact it could be argued that most of life's major journeys are forced upon us. Loved ones die. Divorce and separation occur. Job transfers take us out of the area. Life stages follow one another. Interestingly, most of the journeys recounted in scripture are forced upon individuals: Jacob flees his brother's wrath; Joseph is sold into slavery; Moses escapes punishment in Midian; the Hebrew people escape Egyptian bondage by journeying to the Promised Land; Elijah flees for his life to Horeb; Jesus is "driven" into the wilderness; Paul comes to terms with his Damascus

road experience by going to Arabia. Indeed, even
when our own particular journey seems freely undertaken, as when we give ourselves a weekend to "get
away from it all," we may be equally as compelled—
as "driven"—by spiritual and psychological forces
we do not necessarily comprehend.

CHOOSING A HEALING PLACE

The second major healing component of solitude is
the nature of the place we have chosen to experience
it. Where is it we will seek this healing power of solitude? What place is "right" for us? What place will
be "holy" for us? People frequently cite a sense of
physical expansiveness, great distances visible to the
eye, a sense of remoteness, a place rooted in the lives
of several generations, even a certain quality of the
air, as being important to their awareness of spiritual presence. Places with these and other qualities are
what the Celtic Christians called "thin" places—
places where God breaks more easily into human
consciousness.

Another important element in the healing powers
of solitude is the presence of nature. The woman in
our story retreated to a beach house where the gulls
and even the rocks spoke to her. Most people associate healing with nature, and rightly so. Jeff, for
example, is an employee of a large insurance company in a major city. In his impersonal office cubicle on
the twelfth floor, above his computer terminal and
cluttered desk, is a photograph of the Grand Tetons
of Wyoming where he has often vacationed. Many
times a day Jeff takes a "mini-vacation" by glancing
at his beloved mountains. Gloria is a young woman

in the same office. Each morning on the way to work she walks by a small park. She enjoys observing the park during the different seasons: summer with mothers or grandparents conversing while their children play nearby; fall with the leaves rustling underfoot; winter with its covering of snow; spring with the crocuses pushing up through the moist earth. This park helps make Gloria feel renewed and refreshed as she prepares for her day in the office. Both John and Gloria have discovered the healing power of nature in the heart of the city.

Another important aspect of the choice of place is whether or not, in some sense, it represents "home" to us. Especially in times of crisis, we seek to go home, whether that "home" is a particular place or what author Frederick Buechner calls "a place inside yourself."[2] The woman in our story returns to her "home away from home" at the beach; she also rediscovers her roots in her art, neglected for twenty years. We can find the solitude of home in a variety of places—a neighborhood coffee shop, a nearby church, the local library, even a place where we perform a familiar and well-loved routine, such as swimming laps at the Y. Home is, after all, any place where we feel, if only for a moment, protected, at one with ourselves and in the presence of God. Any such place is a healing spot, a "desert of the heart," if we allow it to become so. Author Margaret Guenther even writes of her regular trips to the blood donor center as an occasion for healing solitude:

I have learned to turn the "empty" two hours of the donation process into a period of intercession....I have come to look forward to my monthly trips to that impersonal, windowless room as a mini-retreat.[3]

SLOWING AND SIMPLIFYING

One of the most important of the healing qualities of solitude is the opportunity to slow down, to step away, if only momentarily, from what author James Gleick calls the "hurry sickness" of our times.[4] The fact is, healing takes time and the element of time itself is one of the most important of the healing elements of solitude. In his poem "The Lake Isle of Innisfree," William Butler Yeats, in words inspired by Thoreau's *Walden,* writes: "I shall have some peace...for peace comes dropping slow." I like that image, that "peace comes dropping slow." In Old Testament times, every fiftieth year was to be a jubilee year in which the land was to lie fallow. There are times when our "land" also needs to lie fallow, when we need to replenish ourselves by not attempting to do anything.

I am struck by how often, in popular art, emotional healing is portrayed by images of waiting. An individual sits alone on a window seat. Two chairs are set, side by side, on a deserted beach. These images reveal what we know instinctively, that one of the healing gifts of solitude is the opportunity to slow down. When we are alone and without distraction, we often find ourselves performing simple actions with a care and an attention that is usually missing from the rest of our life. The more time we spend in solitude, the more we find ourselves center-

ing and focusing, and *in* the centering, *in* the focusing, a healing transformation occurs.

One of the great healing gifts of solitude is also
the opportunity to simplify our lives. Typically when
we experience solitude, we are in a situation in which
our environment is less busy and less demanding
than usual. We may have given ourselves a weekend
away, or we may be on vacation, momentarily disconnected from our fax or e-mail. Or we may be at
home, recuperating from an illness. However we
experience this simplification of our lives, we will
often find it to be a healing experience.

It is no accident that so many religious customs
and practices point in the direction of simplicity of
life: the custom of "giving up something" for Lent;
the traditional manner of keeping the sabbath, in
which work and even daily activities are curtailed;
certainly the monastic vows of poverty. We think of
these customs and traditions as constituting a "sacri-
fice." But could we also think of them as a therapy—
as a means of regaining spiritual and emotional
health? Spiritual writers have traditionally empha-
sized the importance of simplicity of life as a way to
get back in touch with God and with ourselves.
Theophan the Recluse, an appropriately named
Russian monk and bishop of the nineteenth century,
urged his followers toward simplifying their "endless
round of activities," in words that ring even more
true for our own day:

> The chief enemy of life in God is a profusion of
> worldly cares.... When the multitude of cares
> subsides, the mind and heart are left completely
> free.[5]

In our American tradition, one thinks of Henry David Thoreau's famous admonition in *Walden*: "Simplicity, simplicity, simplicity! I say, let your affairs be as two or three, and not a hundred or a thousand."

Achieving simplicity, however, is not easy because it goes against cultural expectations about success. I am reminded of this every time I go to a clergy gathering and hear how other priests greet each other. "How are you?" is inevitably followed by "Busy, busy," as the second individual proceeds to recount a litany of activities and involvements. In my more perverse moments I am tempted to reply, "Oh, I'm not really doing much of anything right now. I have time on my hands. There is really not a lot going on in my church or my life." As much as I am tempted to say this, I know I will not for one simple reason: I am afraid that my colleague might take me seriously and might think of me as less than "successful."

Nevertheless, there are some small, practical ways that we can simplify our lives. One of the most helpful pieces of advice given to me by a wise priest many years ago was that, at a certain point in his day, he would simply tell himself, "I have done enough," and would go home. I remind myself of his words when I am tempted to work to the point of exhaustion. If indeed there is a connection between simplifying one's life and restoring emotional and spiritual harmony, then when we feel the desire to simplify, to pare down, to step back from the "clutter" of our lives, it is important to realize that this is a profoundly healing impulse, and we need to take steps to act upon it.

THE DESIRE FOR HEALING

A final element in the healing power of solitude is to enter it with the specific intention of achieving spiritual and emotional healing. The desire simply to "get away from it all" may be the starting point, but we usually discover that our true intention goes deeper. We need to realize, however, that the healing we seek may not come without a struggle with the dark forces. A story is told of one of the patients of Swiss psychiatrist Carl Jung, who dreamed that he was drowning in a barrel of foul water and refuse. Suddenly above him, in the dream, stood Carl Jung. "Dr. Jung, help me," the man cried. "Get me out." Rather than reaching down to pull him out, Dr. Jung put his foot on the man's shoulder and said, "Not out but through," and thrust him down again into the sewage. Similarly, there are times that our path to healing and wholeness is "not out but through," not to escape from suffering but rather to enter into it and intentionally seek its meaning. Similarly, in *The Genesee Diary* Henri Nouwen recounts the advice given to him by his spiritual director during the course of a seven-month retreat in a Carthusian monastery: "Explore the wounds . . . pay attention to the feelings . . . follow them to their roots."[6]

The fact is, mood disorders and even periods of depression may prove to be ultimately beneficial in that they may point the way to important issues we need to come to terms with in our lives. A question for our whole society, plagued by depression and overprescribed with medications, is that posed by the psalmist so many centuries ago:

Why are you cast down, O my soul,
and why are you disquieted within me?
(Psalm 42:5)

As individuals and as a society, we need to ask ourselves, why *are* our souls so cast down and so disquieted within us? If we can struggle toward an answer to this question, using solitude as part of a journey to self-discovery, we may well experience healing and a renewed sense of purpose. David Awbrey, author of *Finding Hope in the Age of Melancholy,* writes, "Melancholy can be a means to acquire greater truth about life.... Through despair, people can clarify what is important in life, connect themselves to timeless reality."[7]

In our culture, illness often seems to be the method of choice for regaining spiritual and emotional equilibrium. Most of us do not go on spiritual retreats; we do not set apart for ourselves sufficient time for rest and renewal. Instead, the majority of us flog ourselves on until we collapse from mental or physical exhaustion. Therefore, the role of illness needs to be recognized as a means of regaining mental, emotional, and spiritual health. The healing takes place, of course, not primarily during the illness itself but in its aftermath, as we slowly regain our strength. Many individuals remember as one of the most important times in their lives a period when they were recovering from an illness. Even many years later they can recall their pleasure at the simple things of life as they recuperated: a cup of coffee in the morning, the quiet of an empty house, the distant, muffled sounds of the busy world outside. Such occasions, if remembered, remind us of how life *could* be lived, with care and attention to our needs and to the world about us.

In the winter of 1985, shortly after his sixtieth birthday, author William Styron was hospitalized for clinical depression. The combination of alcohol withdrawal and anxiety-producing prescription medications had sent him into a downward spiral of anxiety, insomnia, and an inability to work or concentrate. While in the hospital Styron participated in group therapy but also allowed himself to "waste time." He watched television sitcoms and professional sports, and listened to music. Subsequently Styron wrote of his seven weeks in Yale-New Haven Hospital:

> The hospital was my salvation...a transfer out of the too familiar surroundings of home, where all is anxiety and discord, into an orderly and benign detention.... For me the real healers were seclusion and time.[8]

It is important, however, when speaking of the desire for healing, to realize that this yearning may not necessarily be ours alone. The fact is, we may not know exactly *why* we feel a strong desire to claim some "space" for ourselves. Our motivation may be unclear, even to us. For healing to occur, however, it is sufficient that *God's* intention for us is healing. If we accept God's healing intent for us and are willing to follow where God seems to be leading, including into silence and solitude, then God's healing intent will begin to be manifested in our life.

THE HOLY SPIRIT AND PRAYER

If indeed we experience healing in solitude, if solitude is a neglected path to God, we need to ask, what role does the Holy Spirit play in our desire to seek solitude? At a moment of crisis or transition, when we experience a desire to "get away from it all," is this our own personal desire? Or is the Holy Spirit playing a role?

In order to answer this question, we need to keep in mind the fact that, throughout scripture and the Judeo-Christian tradition, it is usually *God* who pursues *us*. Like Jonah, we are more inclined to flee from God. The role of the Spirit, therefore, becomes first to lead us to that place where we may experience God's presence, and then to reveal to us the particular truth we need to hear. Let us look at this process in more detail.

At a moment of crisis or transition, the Spirit first leads us—"drives" us—into our own particular wilderness, whatever form that takes. This often manifests itself simply as a desire for solitude. But what is occurring is in reality far deeper and more profound than simply the manifestation of a personal desire. It is the Holy Spirit leading us into those places in our own mind and heart—or even, on occasion, those physical places—where we may encounter God's presence. At such a time in our life the Spirit does not give us logical, rational reasons for seeking our own "space," our desert. But once there, often driven there beyond our will, the Spirit then reveals to us "all truth," or at least that aspect of truth we need to encounter. When we receive such an insight, especially one that speaks directly to our own particular situation, we often have the feeling that it came from a source beyond ourselves. "Where did *that* come from?" we ask. The fact is, such insights do not come from us personally. They derive from the Holy Spirit, who leads us into the wilderness for the purpose of gaining insights and direction.

The prayer of silence is one of the great gifts of solitude. Silence is a quality that is missing from our lives most of the time. Most of us live in a world in which objects are constantly ringing at us, beeping for us, and in which other people are constantly clamoring for our attention. Solitude presents the opportunity to reclaim for ourselves—if only for a period of time—the healing gift of prayerful silence. It is significant how often in scripture silence is associated with the presence of God: "Be still, and know that I am God!" (Psalm 46:10); the Lord "leads me beside still waters; he restores my soul" (Psalm 23:2-3); Jesus invites his weary disciples to "come away to a deserted place all by yourselves and rest a while" (Mark 6:31). The traditional religious custom of the silent retreat, now regaining popularity in our own day, is rooted in the healing gift of silence. In solitude, if we are able to resist the temptation to turn on the radio or the television and instead "enter the silence," we will begin to discover its healing power to become prayer.

When we are in crisis, often our first instinct is simply to be alone. We are not, at least at first, seeking "answers." We simply want relief from pain and to regain peace of mind. Such a state of mind is fertile soil for what has been called, in the classic tradition, apophatic spirituality.[9] The Greek word *apophatic* means "negative"; according to this type of spirituality, God is not found through words or images, but through their absence. We must enter God's presence silently, in love. Its spiritual disciplines, in the tradition of Bernard of Clairvaux, include solitude, fasting, and attaining simplicity of life. Apophatic prayer is often wordless, consisting simply of a yearning of the heart, as suggested by Paul's description of prayer in Romans as "sighs too deep for words" (Romans 8:26). When we are in crisis, struggling to achieve a healing of the emotions, we may be surprised to discover that we are engaged in a classic form of spirituality. Nevertheless, this prayer of the heart, as inarticulate as it may be, is often the first step in healing.

There comes a time, however, when the immediate crisis is past and the healing has begun to occur. At this point we begin to seek answers to the questions of life: What do I do now? What is the next step? Where is the path leading me next? We need to formulate plans, decisions, and a course of action. At this stage we move into a different kind of spirituality. *Kataphatic* is a Greek word meaning "affirmative." The goal of kataphatic spirituality is personal spiritual insight and discernment. Its methods include journaling, scripture study, spiritual reading, and deep reflection. The spiritual exercises of St. Ignatius of Loyola belong in this tradition. Kataphatic spirituality leads us back into the world by helping us to see ourselves in a larger context and by formulating a plan of action.

In scripture this approach is suggested by Jesus' question to the two blind men: "What do you want me to do for you?" The point is that they need to articulate their request: "Lord, let our eyes be opened" (Matthew 20:32-33). In a similar fashion, we need also to say exactly *how* we wish to be healed. Personal journaling, contemplation and reflection, and spiritual direction, perhaps following an approach guided by the spiritual exercises of St. Ignatius, can be the means to this end.

It is likely that when we first experience the healing presence of solitude we have in mind no clearly articulated "plan" for achieving healing. We are guided by instinct and need. We almost certainly are not familiar with the names of the classic forms of spirituality, much less what they signify. But as we move spontaneously from the "heart" spirituality of inarticulate yearnings to the "mind" spirituality of spiritual disciplines, we are able to formulate plans and make decisions. These two classic forms of spirituality together provide the healing we need and lead us back into active engagement with the world.

AFTER SOLITUDE:
MAINTAINING THE HEALING

In this chapter we have discussed the healing power of solitude. We have described practical methods for gaining healing and self-insight, for creating, out of our time apart, a "good solitude." It is important now to ask, what do we hope to take out of our solitude when we return, as we inevitably must, to our day-to-day life in the world?

First, we should take with us a new appreciation of the importance of self-nurture. That is something we do not do well in our society: our workaholism reflects our culture's encouragement to put our personal needs last. One of the results of solitude is that we begin to take our needs seriously. We "treat" ourselves gently in small ways as well as in large. Most important, we affirm the importance of self-nurture in general, so we do not lose it when we resume our ordinary life in the world.

Second, solitude provides the opportunity to begin to question the assumptions we live by. We need to ask ourselves, what has brought me to such a state of spiritual and emotional depletion? Henri Nouwen has pointed out that solitude is not simply an opportunity to recharge our batteries and then to go back into the world to live in the same manner that has brought us to the point of spiritual and emotional exhaustion. Instead, solitude presents the opportunity to *challenge the very assumptions we live by*—to begin to live in ways that do not do violence to our spiritual and emotional well-being.[10] Solitude, then, is an opportunity for "repentance"— literally, for "turning again." We turn away from a lifestyle of self-neglect to one of self-nurture. Periods of solitude are not temporary band-aids for continuing and unresolved problems; rather, they point the way toward permanent solutions.

Third, solitude provides the opportunity to begin to develop skills in mental solitude. The fact is, we cannot always "get away" as we might like, or as frequently as we might like. What we *can* do, however, is practice "mental solitude." In speaking of the importance of incorporating silence into one's life, Henri Nouwen uses the image of the storage battery. When we have experienced periods of silence,

Nouwen says, we can then practice *mental* silence. This mental silence is a storage battery, as it were, whose energy we can tap into as we need. In a similar sense, those who have experienced solitude can carry an inner sense of solitude about with them, to renew them and refresh them as needed.[11]

Fourth, solitude gives us the opportunity to define for ourselves the right balance between engagement and renewal, between solitude and community. The fact is that many individuals who feel a strong need for personal renewal have overdosed on involvement. Solitude, however, can also help us discover the opposite: our continuing need for people. Solitude can also renew in us an appreciation for those around us. Intrusive and demanding as they may be, our loved ones share their lives with us, and they must be valued and affirmed. Furthermore, claiming the solitude we need on a regular basis is our gift to them as well as to ourselves; when *we* are renewed and refreshed, then we can be fully present to them when we return.

Finally, solitude provides the opportunity to continue our process of personal self-discovery. Typically in our solitude we have taken preliminary steps toward self-discovery. We have gathered some hints—some intimations—of who we are as unique individuals, of what our "life mission" might consist, of what shape our "vocation" might take. Now we need to continue this ongoing process of self-discovery. In the next chapter we focus on the role of solitude in the rediscovery of the self.

QUESTIONS FOR REFLECTION

1. Recollect a time when you needed spiritual or emotional healing. Did you seek out people for help, or time alone, or some combination of the two? Which proved most helpful? Did solitude enable you to integrate insights gained from others?

2. Have you ever sought the healing a change of environment can bring? What were the circumstances? Where did you go? How did physical or psychological distancing assist in your healing?

3. Do you find that simplifying your life is an aid to healing? What specific steps could you take to simplify your life further? Where would you begin? What internal or external forces are keeping you from simplifying? How could they be overcome?

4. Recall a time of prayer or reflection that was especially meaningful for you. What was the setting? Were you alone or with others? Did you spend the time in silence, in worship, or in seeking some form of rational understanding? What does this suggest to you about the form of prayer (conventional or unconventional) that is best suited for you?

CHAPTER FOUR

Solitude and the Self

Who am I? Do I have an identifiable self? Self-knowledge is part of wisdom, but what is this "self" we seek to know? How can we be true to the "self"?

Attaining a sense of identity is arguably more difficult today than ever before. While in past centuries the circumstances in which we were born largely determined our identity, today people have the opportunity to reinvent themselves, that is, to form a series of new identities throughout life. The Internet even provides the opportunity to invent a new identity with a few keystrokes. Baby boomers, now moving into their forties and fifties, are encountering identity-changing circumstances as they become "the older generation": the empty nest, divorce or separation, new jobs or careers, caring for aging parents. Amidst changing circumstances people wonder whether there *is* a bedrock "self." Is our identity nothing more than a series of roles we assume throughout life?

Our society tends to discourage the reflectiveness that might lead to answers to this question. As a result many of us lack clarity about who we are and what we want out of life. The best-selling book *Tuesdays with Morrie* recounts a moving dialogue between a dying college professor and his former student Mitch, a fast-track newspaper reporter struggling to understand the meaning and purpose of his life:

> "Mitch," he said, "the culture doesn't encourage you to think about such things until you're about to die. We're so wrapped up with egotistical things, career, family, having enough money, meeting the mortgage, getting a new car, fixing the radiator when it breaks—we're involved in trillions of little acts just to keep going. So we don't get into the habit of standing back and looking at our lives and saying, Is this all? Is this all I want? Is something missing?" He paused. "You need someone to probe you in that direction. It won't just happen automatically."[1]

Not only does our society discourage reflection, it discourages us from asking what is perhaps the ultimate question: What is the purpose of being true to ourselves and of discovering our identity? Is it simply to achieve self-expression? Or is there something beyond that? Is the purpose nothing less than our discovery of what has been called, in the religious tradition, our vocation, our calling or life mission? Is self-discovery not in fact the means by which we identify the particular path of service to which God is leading us?

However we wish to conceive of the purpose of discovering our "identity," the fact is, it often takes a major shock or dislocation for us to become truly reflective. And often at such times we either seek solitude or it is thrust upon us. This is what happened to the prophet Elijah, one of the most fascinating figures of the Old Testament. Elijah can be a paradigm for people of our own day who use solitude to attain a sense of clarity and personal meaning.

We meet Elijah in the sixteenth chapter of the first book of Kings. Israel has fallen into apostasy: the king of Israel has married a Phoenician woman, Jezebel, and has imported pagan practices into the palace itself. Elijah speaks out against this desecration and even, in a bold move, slays the pagan prophets of the queen. As a result, the words of Jezebel are reported back to Elijah: "So may the gods do to me, and more also, if I do not make your life like the life of one of them by this time tomorrow" (1 Kings 19:2). Now Elijah is in danger for his life.

At this point he embarks on a very wise course of action. He flees to the wilderness. He is fleeing not only for his life, but also in search of something else—for we read that he flees to Horeb, the "mount of God" (1 Kings 19:8). Horeb is another name for Sinai, the mountain where Elijah's spiritual ancestor, Moses, received the Ten Commandments. Elijah flees into the wilderness for the purpose of going "home"—home not only to his own spiritual roots but also to the spiritual roots of his whole people.

Upon arriving at Sinai, Elijah lodges in a cave and, shortly after, some very strange events take place.

> [The LORD] said, "Go out and stand on the mountain before the LORD, for the LORD is about to pass by." Now there was a great wind, so strong that it was splitting mountains and breaking rocks in pieces before the LORD, but the LORD was not in the wind; and after the wind an earthquake, but the LORD was not in the earthquake; and after the earthquake a fire, but the LORD was not in the fire. (1 Kings 19:11-12)

What are we to make of this story? Perhaps we could see the earthquake, the wind, and the fire as symbols of the chaotic nature of life—not only Elijah's but our own as well. Sometimes our lives *feel* like an earthquake, a wind, and a fire. And *in* this chaos, the clarity we seek—the sense of God's presence—seems to elude us.

But Elijah perseveres. What happens next for Elijah is a moment of revelation. After the chaos of the earthquake, wind, and fire, Elijah steps outside his cave and finally hears "a sound of sheer silence" (1 Kings 19:12). Other translations call it a "still, small voice." At the climax of the story, Elijah receives some very specific directives. He is to carry out the prophet's task of anointing Kings—Hazael over Syria and Jehu over Israel—and to pass the prophetic mantle along to his own successor, Elisha.

After receiving his marching orders, Elijah goes down from his mountain, performs all the actions the LORD commands, joins forces with the seven thousand men who have been there all along, and saves the nation of Israel for another day. He also assures that the word of the LORD will continue to be heard in Israel.

What does this story of Elijah say to us today? How can we use Elijah's story as a paradigm for contemporary men and women who seek revelation, and therefore personal clarity, in their own lives? First, we might perceive the story of Elijah as an allegory for ourselves when we become discouraged and lose a sense of who we are and what God wants us to do. At such a moment in his own life Elijah instinctively does the right thing. He seeks his "home," his spiritual "roots." He seeks his "center"—not only his own, but the worship center of his whole people— Sinai, the Mount of God. Elijah reminds us that what we personally seek is also connected to the spiritual forces that have shaped us, to the values of the spiritual community of which we are part. We need to reconnect with our own depths and with the values and traditions of the faith communities which have formed us.

Second, Elijah's spiritual journey is not easy. Just because he *seeks* clarity does not mean he immediately finds it. The road to revelation and insight leads first through the earthquake, the wind, and the fire. This is an important part of the story. We need to be reminded that revelation and insight will occur in their own time. We need to be patient.

Third, Elijah finally does hear the "sound of sheer silence." This does not happen in the earthquake, the wind, and the fire. When our lives are too crazy, too chaotic, too overburdened, the clarity we seek will elude us. As much as we may *want* to make decisions and plans for the future, those we make in a state of chaos will almost certainly turn out wrong. In order to decide wisely, we need to get ourselves on the other side of the earthquake, wind, and fire before we hear God's "still, small voice."

Finally, Elijah receives some very specific directions. Here at last is the clarity Elijah seeks—the clarity *we* seek in our own lives. But—and this is the point—such clarity comes only *after* we have settled ourselves emotionally and spiritually. It comes after the earthquake, wind, and fire. It is only then that we hear the still, small voice, and receive the clarity we seek.

One example of a contemporary seeker is Paul Hawker, author of *Soul Survivor: A Spiritual Quest Through 40 Days and 40 Nights of Mountain Solitude.* Hawker, a successful forty-three-year-old New Zealand television producer, found himself increasingly aware of something important missing in his life. He writes:

> Like many middle-class white males, I've had a fortuitous life with all the trappings of what society would deem success.... Yet despite all this there was something missing, not quite right, a restlessness, a yearning. Without warning I'd be overcome by despair. Seemingly from nowhere, wave after wave of melancholy would wash over me and then recede, leaving me feeling alone,

hollow, and a fraud. A part of me was missing, but I had no idea what it was. It was so deeply buried and long lost I could no longer identify it.[2]

While in the depths of his midlife malaise, a friend gives him the suggestion he needs: "Sounds like you need a wilderness experience, mate: 40 days and 40 nights." Accordingly, Hawker packs his bags and sets off for Arête, a mountain that had attracted him with its outrageous beauty as a young man twenty-two years before. Like Elijah, Hawker goes to the mountain to find himself. Like Elijah (and Jesus), Hawker spends forty days on his spiritual quest.

As the days unfold in solitude on the mountain of his youth, Hawker experiences various changes and transformations—physical, emotional, and spiritual. The question that had brought him to the mountain, however—rooting his "career" in a deeper sense of vocation—continues to elude him. One day Hawker has a chance meeting with a Dutch mountaineer:

> I shared with him my reasons for being there, and some of the things I'd experienced. I told him that I'd done everything I'd ever wanted to do and I wasn't sure what to do next. That I had lost touch with who I was, why I was on earth, and where I was heading. I had lost my way and with it much of my passion for life. He was quite surprised: "But you have an incredible passion to tell, it just flows out of you!" Bingo! It was as if someone had turned on the floodlights. The mist of my confusion instantly evaporated. Here, completely out of the blue, was an affirmation of my passion, of who I really was. Edwin was

right! I loved telling. From the time I was a small boy when my patient mother listened to my tall tales, to my work as a filmmaker, I reveled in telling. I love stories. I love processing and reworking information, reassembling it so it's more readily understood. It's who I am. I'd simply die if I couldn't tell it![3]

At this moment, Hawker, like Elijah, rediscovers his core identity in a context of silence, solitude, and wilderness. It happens through his contact with the Dutch mountaineer, who relates to Hawker almost as a spiritual guide or director. As a result, like Elijah, Hawker is able to rededicate himself to his life work, reenergized and reconfirmed in who he is and what he does.

Solitude plays a major role in stories like these. Like so many other individuals in scripture—Joseph, Hagar, Jacob, Moses, Paul, certainly Jesus himself—Elijah comes to the truth about himself in the wilderness. Could Elijah perhaps have experienced the same clarity, the same self-insight, *away* from the wilderness? Perhaps. But for Elijah, for Paul Hawker, and I suspect for most of us, solitude *in some form* provides the fertile ground for deep reflection.

SOLITUDE AND COMMUNITY

It is often said that we discover who we are in community. And yet Elijah and many others in scripture *leave* community to discover who they are in the solitude of the wilderness. How do we reconcile the paradox of solitude versus community in gaining insight?

I personally believe that we *do* discover who we are in community. Our understanding of vocation and ministry in the church, for example, is rooted in the belief that it is the community that commissions us to pursue a particular path of service. In fact, the validity of our personal sense of call is tested by whether or not the community also perceives the validity of the call. In my own life, I remember how my call to be a preacher of the gospel was validated and affirmed by the reaction of my own congregation to the preaching of my first sermon during my first year of seminary. But we often come to terms with what that means in solitude. Community and solitude are in continuous dialogue with each other in the process of self-discovery.

When we discuss the role of a community in shaping identity, however, one important caveat needs to be stated: the identity formed "in community" is not necessarily an accurate reflection of who we really are. One thinks of individuals whose self-esteem has been damaged, sometimes for life, by a dysfunctional family of origin, or by emotional or physical abuse by their peers. One thinks also of women and peoples whose self-perceptions historically have been affected adversely by prevailing social attitudes. So yes, we discover who we are (or who we think we are) "in community." But what we discover is not unambiguous in nature, nor does it necessarily reflect our true self. At some point and in some circumstances, we may need to step outside our community of origin to discover who we *really* are.

In the story of Abraham in Genesis, his separation from his community of origin is linked to God's call to him to be a "blessing" for others:

> Now the LORD said to Abram, "Go from your country and your kindred and your father's house to the land that I will show you. I will make of you a great nation, and I will bless you." (Genesis 12:1-2)

A contemporary example is that of Joan Anderson, a middle-aged woman with grown children and a marriage lacking in intimacy, who writes of taking a year to live by herself on the Massachusetts coast. During the course of this year she reflects on the various "identities" she has carried as wife and mother:

> It was more or less expected that a woman would create relationship first and herself second. . . . Of primary importance now is for me to retrieve the buried parts of me—qualities like playfulness, vulnerability, being at home in my skin, using more of my instincts. Like so many pieces of a puzzle, I need to find a way to create the whole once again.[4]

Anderson is subsequently able to renew her relationship with her husband, but now with a sure sense of who she is and how she wishes to live in relationship.

Why does a sense of personal clarity appear to emerge in solitude? What special qualities of solitude seem conducive to evoking personal insight and reflection? Why do so many individuals in scripture either achieve personal clarity or struggle with issues relating to it in solitude? Certainly one reason is the absence of distractions when we are alone. For the moment we are away from all those other voices clamoring for our attention. One of my favorite songs of the sixties begins with the lines, "Everybody's talkin' at me. I can't hear a word they're sayin'." The message is found in the preposition *at*. For most of us most of the time, people *are* constantly talking "at" us—our bosses, family members, the radio and television, and all the advertisements with their message that our self-worth is measured by how we look and the things we own. In this cacophony, we can barely hear our own voice, much less the "still, small voice" of God within us. Solitude gives us the opportunity to enter for a period of time our own particular "desert," of which theologian Kenneth Leech writes:

> In the desert we are deprived of those things which prevent us from seeing ourselves and reality in nakedness and simplicity, freed from disguises and false appearances. We are reduced to a simplicity of life and set free from attachments which obstruct our path. So we begin to see more clearly.[5]

The most important quality of solitude, however, is that it represents what author Richard Rohr calls a "liminal space."[6] The word "liminal," from the Latin *limen,* or threshold, denotes not only the boundary between two distinct spaces or states of being. It also signifies the threshold into a totally new space and therefore carries with it a sense of mystery and of the unexpected. Therefore, we encounter extraordinary creativity in liminal space. You and I experience a liminal space when we go on retreat or on vacation and find ourselves for the moment somewhat disoriented. In this very disorientation, creative insights seem to emerge. The experience of solitude, especially if following a busy, active period of life, can be a liminal space. It is interesting to note that the Hebrew concept of work embraced not only the work itself, but also the necessary rest and relaxation *away* from work—the liminal space between tasks, so to speak. A music critic once remarked that more than half of Beethoven is silence. Beethoven's notes take their meaning from the silence that surrounds them. Solitude provides the opportunity to step back, emotionally and spiritually, to reassess and re-vision and, in so doing, to begin to move toward a regained sense of personal clarity.

REVELATION AND CLARITY: FOR WHAT PURPOSE?

If revelation and personal clarity can emerge as the result of solitude, we need to ask, clarity about what and for what purpose? How does personal clarity lead to a closer relation with God and with ourselves as children of God?

On the simplest level, solitude gives us the opportunity to become clear about our own needs. We cannot truly love and serve God unless our own basic needs are met. As a result of solitude, we rediscover our emotional, physical, and spiritual requirements for health and wholeness. "Surely we are aware of our own needs," we say. Sadly, this is in fact not the case; if it were we would not do such violence to ourselves and to our own basic needs on a daily basis. Caregivers in particular—mothers of young children, women juggling family and work, members of the helping professions—all routinely ignore their own needs in the interests of serving others. Such individuals need to be reminded that they cannot adequately serve others if they are not whole themselves, and solitude can be a way to get back in touch with basic requirements of emotional, physical, and spiritual health.

Solitude can also begin the process of reconciling the split between our inner and outer selves, bringing us ultimately to a more focused relation to God. Probably all of us experience the separation between inner and outer selves to one degree or another. Scripture speaks of the individual who is "double-minded" and therefore "unstable in every way" (James 1:8). Most people living in the modern world experience this double-mindedness, or even triple- or quadruple-mindedness on a daily basis. Anne Morrow Lindbergh well expresses the desire of many people to reconcile the split between the inner and outer when she writes of her intentions in spending time in solitude at the beach in *Gift from the Sea:*

> I want first of all . . . to be at peace with myself. I want a singleness of eye, a purity of intention, a central core to my life. . . . I want, in fact—to borrow from the language of the saints—to live "in grace" as much of the time as possible. . . . By grace I mean an inner harmony, essentially spiritual, which can be translated into outward harmony. I am seeking perhaps what Socrates asked for in the prayer from the *Phaedrus* when he said,

"May the outward and inward man be at one." I would like to achieve a state of inner spiritual grace from which I could function and give as I was meant to in the eye of God.[7]

In solitude we may also gain clarity about our own particular vocation—our calling or life mission. It is fascinating to me how often in scripture solitude is associated with the issue of identity. The young Joseph of the Old Testament is alone in the desert when he is asked by a mysterious stranger, "What are you seeking?" At seventeen, Joseph does not "hear" the portentousness of this question. Instead he responds with his immediate concern: "I am seeking my brothers... Tell me please, where they are pasturing the flock" (Genesis 37:15-16). One may surmise that only years later, in the maturity of adulthood, is Joseph able to realize that what he was really "seeking" as a young man in the desert was a way of reconciling the grandiose dreams of youth with an adult path of service in the world.

Whether our own self-discovery begins in solitude, as did Joseph's, or is intentionally sought in solitude, as with Elijah and Jesus, solitude gives us the "space" to begin to discover the particular mission to which we are called. The early church called this process of discernment leading to insight *diakrisis*, and believed that it was especially nurtured by silence and solitude.

The discovery or rediscovery of the self may occur at any time during life, but midlife is especially fertile terrain. Furthermore, what we often discover at such times in our life is not that we have followed the wrong path entirely. It is rather that we have lost sight of the path that was ours all along. We have allowed ourselves to be distracted by other concerns, involvements, and responsibilities. An insight that this is the case is the first stop in reclaiming our true path or in discovering an entirely new path of service to God.

In 1946 a young nun was on a train from Calcutta to Darjeeling to make a religious retreat. She had come to India from her native Yugoslavia to begin work in the Bengali Mission of the Loretto Sisters at the age of nineteen. She was happy in her new work, taking her first vows two years later and her final vows six years after that. On the train to the Himalayas, however, she had an experience that would change her life and the lives of many others:

> She felt a "call within a call." "It was," she reflected, "a vocation to give up even Loretto where I was very happy and to go out into the streets to serve the poorest of the poor. . . . I heard the call to give up all and follow [Christ] into the slums to serve him among the poorest of the poor." She applied for the necessary permissions to leave the convent and strike out on her own. Two years later all the official approvals had come through. Mother Teresa left the beautiful garden and "the quiet peaceful place" that had been her religious home. She walked out alone into the streets of Calcutta.[8]

In a similar way, Henri Nouwen writes of his own insight concerning his vocation at the end of seven months living in a Trappist monastery:

It seems that my retreat has affirmed and deep-
ened an already existing trend. What is becoming
clear is the need to enter into [my own special
vocation of writing, speaking, and teaching]
more deeply, more fully, more extremely.[9]

Finally, in solitude we may become clear about
our own gifts as they relate to the scriptural commands that all Christians are to "serve one another
with whatever gift each of you has received" (1 Peter
4:10). The first step is to *discover* one's gift. The second is to *use* one's gift for the benefit of others. The
fact is, scripture has no conception of the use of one's
gifts purely for "self-expression," in a contemporary
sense. Rather, gifts are given to individuals "for the
common good" (1 Corinthians 12:7), that is, to serve
the larger community. Those individuals in scripture
who gained insight in solitude—Elijah, Moses, Paul,
Jesus—returned to the world to live out their new
sense of vocation. Ultimately the insights we gain in
solitude give us a renewed sense of dedication to living out our vocation in the world. But this personal
sense of vocation, and an understanding of how it
relates to the needs of the world, originates in the
"desert" of our own hearts.

This moment of clarity may be manifested in a
variety of ways. It may come suddenly in the form of
a startling insight following a long period of reflection, or struggle, around a particular issue in our
lives. It may be triggered by a friend's chance remark
that just "feels right." It may come in the form of a
dream, startling in its revelation and insight into the
nature of our circumstances. Whatever form this revelation takes, such moments are often described as

"aha" experiences. Individuals remark subsequently that they simply "knew" what they needed to do. Such experiences carry with them a powerful sense of validity, along with absolute clarity. We may subsequently remark, "I can't believe I never saw this before." The fact is, it takes years of experience, as well as a degree of distancing, before we receive such a revelation, which, in retrospect, seems so "obvious."

What role does *actual* solitude play in such moments of revelation? As we have remarked previously, solitude typically functions in one of two ways. It may be the *setting* in which the moment of revelation finally occurs, as with Anne Morrow Lindbergh. Or it may be the *means* by which individuals come to terms with a revelation that has already occurred, as it was with Henri Nouwen on retreat at the monastery. Since human experience is complex by nature and seldom conforms to simple either-or criteria, solitude for most of us may be *both* the setting for the original revelation *and* the means by which we work it out. Furthermore, the "solitude" to which I refer may not necessarily be a *literal* solitude, but may be that "liminal space" removed from one's ordinary reality. Whatever form this liminal space takes in our lives, solitude—*actual* solitude—may play a major role.

QUESTIONS FOR REFLECTION

1. Do you believe that each of us has a core self sparate from the various roles we play? What adjectives would you use to describe your core self? How is it sometimes in conflict with your various roles?

2. Recall a time that you, like Elijah, fled to the "wilderness" to rediscover yourself. What form did this wilderness take? What did you discover about yourself and about God's path for you? Were you subsequently able to incorporate your insights into your life?

3. Describe a time when a community of which you were part called you to a particular task or to a new understanding of yourself. Describe another time when your community discouraged you from pursuing the right path. Which type of experience has been more common for you? Would you say, in general, that community has played a positive or a negative role in your self-discovery?

4. This chapter speaks of the importance of bringing our inner and outer selves into harmony. Which parts of yourself do you currently see as being in harmony? In conflict? What specific steps could you take to resolve a conflict with which you are currently struggling?

CHAPTER FIVE

Solitude and Temperament

It would be difficult to imagine two such different personalities as Michael and Carole. Both are members of Trinity Church. Church and serve as members of the parish's outreach committee. Michael, a psychologist in his late thirties, is the executive director of a community mental health agency with three locations, soon to be expanding to a fourth. He is constantly on the go, his days filled with phone calls, committee meetings, and consultations with clients. Michael thrives on constant engagement and cannot imagine any other way to live. He pours this same energy into his role as chair of the parish outreach committee: under his leadership this formerly moribund committee has trans-

formed itself into a powerhouse of energy and commitment. Through the outreach committee the parish
is now involved in providing affordable housing for
low-income families, sponsoring an after-school
tutorial program, and spearheading a drive for a
community food bank.

A widow in her early fifties, Carole is the clerk of
the outreach committee. After two hours of
Michael's whirlwind energy at committee meetings,
Carole looks forward to withdrawing to her study at
the rear of her house and transcribing the minutes.
Carole is fed by moments of quiet reflection. Every
day she looks forward to a period of "alone time" in
her study, looking out into the woods at the back of
her house and watching the late afternoon sunlight
slanting through the trees.

Michael and Carole like each other and they
appreciate each other's very different work on the
committee, but they do not understand each other.
Michael cannot imagine a life as quiet and withdrawn as Carole's seems to be; Carole cannot imagine a life as constantly on-the-go as Michael's. One
afternoon when she spent an hour in Michael's office
discussing committee business, she was jarred by the
constant interruptions of the phone ringing and co-
workers popping in every five minutes to ask a question. Again, Michael seemed energized by all this
frantic activity while Carole was depleted by it.
When their meeting was over, Carole went home and
went to bed and Michael went on to a school board
meeting.

The fundamental difference between Michael and
Carole is their very different requirements for soli-

tude. Solitude plays virtually no part in Michael's life. Even away from the job, Michael is constantly *with* others: a family trip to Disneyworld, basketball at the Y, periodic reunions with his high school and college buddies. Carole, however, thrives on solitude. Her peaceful house on the edge of the woods is a haven. Carole hungers for and seeks out solitude; Michael hungers for and seeks out involvement with other people.

Michael and Carole often joke that even their spiritual disciplines reflect their different temperaments. Carole is drawn to meditation and quiet reflection. Her morning devotion focuses on such scriptural passages as "For God alone my soul waits in silence." For Carole the quiet moments before the Sunday service and the times of silent prayer during the service itself are especially rich. She also looks forward to the annual parish retreat, which provides ample time for reading and reflection between the scheduled meditations. And yet Carole wonders if sometimes she becomes too reclusive, avoiding the painful stretching life in community can bring.

Michael's faith, on the other hand, is centered on his experience of the community of faith and the fellowship of believers. The principal service on Sunday, in which the entire community is gathered in celebration, is the highlight of Michael's spiritual life. He especially enjoys the passing of the peace during the service. Special parish events, especially those that involve people serving together like the Annual Men's Group breakfast, are occasions when Michael's faith seems most "real." And yet there are times that Michael wonders whether his life is lived too much on the surface. He senses that there are parts of himself that he has not discovered, much less lived out. Sometimes he even wonders whether Carole's path of quiet reflection might contain the answers he is seeking.

The presence of two such opposite temperaments in people like Michael and Carole, as well as a whole range of temperaments in between, presents a challenge to every parish community. The Michaels of the faith community will respond to opportunities for involvement with others; the Caroles will seek to go deeper in faith by cultivating their inner world. They will therefore be drawn to different opportunities for involvement, different preaching styles, and even different forms of prayer. The challenge for church leaders, therefore, is to be conscious of this difference, and to be intentional about making a range of opportunities for people of very different temperaments available in each parish.

The stories of Michael and Carole demonstrate some of the difficulties we have with solitude today. People like Michael neglect solitude because they are not instinctively drawn to it and because society does not encourage the pursuit of it. More inward people like Carole are often made to feel guilty for their attraction to solitude. And yet solitude is a path to God for both Carole and Michael. For Carole it is her natural milieu, the place where she feels God's presence most strongly. For Michael it is where he senses he may find the answers he is seeking.

What makes Michael and Carole so different? Why is it that what feeds and energizes Michael depletes Carole? Why do they have such different requirements for solitude? Furthermore, in spite of these differences, is it possible that even Michael needs renewal and solitude from time to time? Is it possible that Carole needs more engagement and contact with a community? Finally, what can we learn from Michael's and Carole's very different lifestyles that we can apply to our own lives in seeking to understand our own need for solitude and renewal?

The fundamental difference between Michael and Carole is one of *temperament*. Michael is one of the estimated seventy-five percent of the general population who are *extroverts*, individuals who are strongly drawn to the world outside themselves. Carole is one of the estimated twenty-five percent who are *introverts*, nourished by an inner world of thoughts and feelings. The concepts of introversion and extroversion to denote differing temperaments were developed by psychologist Carl Jung almost one hundred years ago and have since been further refined by depth psychologists.[1]

Extroverts, like Michael, are energized by involvement with others. They can easily deal with interruptions and in fact often welcome them. They crave variety, activity, and engagements with many people, even if only on a superficial basis. The character of Mr. Toad in Kenneth Grahame's classic story *The Wind in the Willows,* with his cry, "Travel, change, interest, excitement! The world constantly before you ... " is the cry of the consummate extrovert. In contrast, introverts such as Carole are oriented to their inner world of thoughts and feelings. They are energized by being alone. Although they enjoy carefully selected relationships with others, they crave quiet, time to think and reflect, and the solitude in which to do it.

We have said that the difference between Michael and Carole is one of temperament. It is important to note that temperament is different from personality, although the two words are often used interchangeably. The origin of the word "personality" is the Greek word *persona,* referring to the masks that Greek actors wore. It suggests that what we call personality relates primarily to the *social* self, that is, the self that we present to others, formed by the social and cultural conditioning we have received throughout life. Our concept of *temperament,* on the other hand, has its origin not in the idea of social conditioning, but rather in biology. Rooted originally in the ancient belief in the existence of "humors"— bodily fluids whose mixture supposedly determined mood, behavior, and mental outlook—the concept of temperament represents an early attempt to identify the biological roots of behavior and the nature of the self.

To use the imperfect analogy of a computer, personality is our individual software, the "program" that social and cultural forces have created for us and that, on some level, we "choose" to play. Temperament, on the other hand, is our hard drive. It is the manner and style with which we play the "program" of personality, along with other biological determinants of behavior, such as our innate energy level and our basic emotional and physical health.

If temperament is the biological basis upon which personality rests, then what does this say about our concept of individuality? We tend to assume that all people are basically alike and we have a "right" to express ourselves differently, to choose to "do our own thing," so to speak. But what if doing our own thing is not so much a choice as a biological and spiritual necessity? What if we are in fact different from each other in important and significant ways? What if we perceive our environment differently, process ideas differently, learn differently, and possess very different requirements for such qualities as solitude and time for renewal? Furthermore, what if such differences are not only biological and social, but also spiritual in nature?

If this is the case, then we need to take such differences seriously; we need to accept them and to act upon them. Michael and Carole, for example, do not "choose" to act so differently and to express such different lifestyles. Rather, Michael and Carole *are* in fact different and are inevitably expressing their very different natures through their very different lifestyles. It also means that we are called to do the same in our own lives. How might we come to accept, appreciate, and nurture our different temperaments and requirements for solitude?

MARY AND MARTHA

Although the Hebrew and Christian scriptures have no articulated theory of personality or temperament in a modern psychological sense, they are full of stories that dramatize the very different ways that the people of God have acted according to their unique

temperaments and gifts. Temperamental differences,
for example, are dramatically illustrated by the story
of Mary and Martha in the tenth chapter of Luke's
gospel. As a parish priest, I know Mary and Martha
very well. I see them every day in my life in the
church.

Mary, her sister Martha, and their brother
Lazarus were apparently personal friends of Jesus.
During Jesus' last days, before he entered Jerusalem
for the final time, Jesus visited them in their home in
Bethany, a tiny village outside Jerusalem:

> He entered a certain village, where a woman
> named Martha welcomed him into her home. She
> had a sister named Mary, who sat at the Lord's
> feet and listened to what he was saying. But
> Martha was distracted by her many tasks; so she
> came to him and asked, "Lord, do you not care
> that my sister has left me to do all the work by
> myself? Tell her then to help me." But the Lord
> answered her, "Martha, Martha, you are worried
> and distracted by many things; there is need of
> only one thing. Mary has chosen the better part,
> which will not be taken away from her." (Luke
> 10:38-42)

This portrayal of Mary as reflective by nature and
perhaps inclined to avoid practical necessities and of
Martha as busy with the affairs of the world is
echoed by John's account of the circumstances sur-
rounding the subsequent death of their brother
Lazarus. Mary and Martha send word to Jesus that
Lazarus is gravely ill and presumably near death.
Jesus travels with his disciples to their village of

Bethany, where he is met outside the house by Martha, who informs him that Lazarus has died and is already in the tomb. In this situation of family crisis, we note that it is typically the can-do Martha who immediately takes charge:

> When Martha heard that Jesus was coming, she went and met him, while Mary stayed at home. Martha said to Jesus, "Lord, if you had been here, my brother would not have died." (John 11:20-21)

Mary, however, is mourning inside the house and has to be told, "The Teacher is here and is calling for you" (11:28).

We see reflected in these two gospel accounts of Mary and Martha a picture of two of temperaments. Martha, the active one, busies herself serving the food and takes charge of a family crisis; Mary, who is more inward, instead sits at the feet of Jesus listening to his teachings, and, later, mourns the death of her brother in private. Each offers a different gift: Martha, the gift of hospitality; Mary, herself as a disciple. Mary and Martha also demonstrate the shadow side of their respective temperaments. Mary may be, we suspect, ineffectual at times, too inclined to retreat from the hustle and bustle of the world. And Martha runs the danger of becoming overly caught up—consumed, as it were—by external circumstances and responsibilities. Various translations of Luke's gospel describe her as "worried and distracted," "worried and upset," "worried and bothered," "anxious and troubled," "fretting and fussing" and "upset over...details." These are clearly descriptions of an individual who has, for the moment, lost a sense of herself—always a danger for strong and hospitable personalities with a sense of responsibility for others.

On the simplest level, the story of Mary and Martha can be seen as the portrayal of two very different temperaments—temperaments we all recognize from our own acquaintances: the withdrawn, reflective Mary and the can-do, busy Martha. On a deeper level, however, Mary and Martha can be perceived as the two sides of our own temperament: our need, on the one hand, periodically to withdraw and reflect, and on the other, to be actively involved in the affairs of the world. Seen in this way, the story reminds us that both are necessary but that each is sometimes in conflict with the other. In the words of Theophan the Recluse:

> There are two ways to become one with God: the active way and the contemplative way. . . . But in practice neither way can exist in total isolation from the other. Those who live in the world must also keep to the contemplative way in some measure.[2]

Jesus' remark that Mary has "chosen the better part" can be seen as an attempt to correct the balance, to compensate for the attitude of the world that tends to approve of the Marthas while disparaging the Marys' need to withdraw and take stock. Most of us, in other words, live out our busy Martha side of involvement in the world but have to be reminded to live out Mary's reflective side as well.

However, there is also another possible interpretation of Jesus' words. He may be referring *only* to Mary's situation. He may be saying, in effect, Mary has chosen "the better part" *for her*. That is, for Mary with her introverted nature, the "better part" for her is to sit quietly at the feet of Jesus. Understood in this fashion, Jesus' words are an affirmation of *true* individuality, reminding us that we are in fact different from each other in temperament and that our different natures require different ways of living in the world.

MOSES AND JETHRO

As the rector of an Episcopal parish as well as an introvert who is called to lead, I have always identified with the story of Moses and Jethro. It reminds me of the pitfalls of leadership for an introvert like myself and of what I need to do to remain balanced and effective. Moses reminds me that my particular temperament is a gift from God, but also that it presents potential dangers as well as opportunities.

The portrait of Moses that emerges from the account of his calling in Exodus and of a crisis in his leadership in Numbers suggests a strongly inward individual. Exodus tells the story of how Moses, as a young man, becomes enraged by the beating of a Hebrew, one of his own people, by an Egyptian. Moses kills the oppressor and flees to the wilderness, where he is befriended by Jethro, a "priest of Midian." Moses marries one of Jethro's daughters and becomes a shepherd for his new father-in-law. Exodus states that Moses is "content" to dwell with Jethro (Exodus 2:21, RSV). One wonders, is this

contentment only that of a newly married man as
well as one relieved to have escaped possible criminal
persecution? Or is it also something more—a recognition that the solitary life of a shepherd speaks
deeply to the needs of his particular temperament? In
any case Moses is alone tending his flock when God's
revelation comes to him in the burning bush (Exodus
3:1-2). When the Lord calls him to assume a highly
public role as the leader of the Hebrew people out of
their bondage in Egypt, his first reaction is one of
active resistance: "O my Lord, please send someone
else" (Exodus 4:13). Even the nature of the regard
with which Moses was held, that "the LORD used to
speak to Moses face to face, as one speaks to a
friend" (Exodus 33:11), seems to reflect a recognition of some unusual depth of spirituality—again, a
characteristic many would ascribe to an inward-ori-
ented temperament.

What happens, however, when someone like
Moses is called to a public position of leadership?
After the Hebrew people had fled from slavery in
Egypt and while they were in the wilderness, Moses,
following the custom of the time, functioned as his
people's judge and legislator as well as their military
and religious leader. This required Moses to settle
grievances between individuals and periodically to sit
in judgment as people presented their disputes to
him. Probably nothing is more draining and frustrat-
ing for an introvert than to deal with conflict and the
settling of personal disputes. One can hear the depth
of his frustration as he complains to the Lord:

> Why have you treated your servant so badly?
> Why have I not found favor in your sight, that

you lay the burden of all this people on me? Did
I conceive all this people? Did I give birth to
them? . . . If this is the way you are going to treat
me, put me to death at once—if I have found
favor in your sight—and do not let me see my
misery. (Numbers 11:11-12, 15)

Moses's father-in-law Jethro observes him judging
the people and then reveals his own deep intuitive
sense of human nature, as well as of the psychological limits of his introverted son-in-law, when he confronts Moses with the nature of his problem:

What is this that you are doing for the people?
Why do you sit alone, while all the people stand
around you from morning until evening? . . .
What you are doing is not good. You will surely
wear yourself out, both you and these people
with you. For the task is too heavy for you; you
cannot do it alone. (Exodus 18:14, 17-18)

Then Jethro proposes a common sense solution:

Look for able men among all the people, men
who fear God, are trustworthy, and hate dishon-
est gain; set such men over them as officers over
thousands, hundreds, fifties and tens. Let them
sit as judges for the people at all times; let them
bring every important case to you, but decide
every minor case themselves. So it will be easier
for you, and they will bear the burden with you.
If you do this, and God so commands you, then
you will be able to endure, and all these people
will go to their home in peace. (Exodus 18:21-
23)

Jethro encourages Moses to share the burden of leadership. He is still an introvert, but now he is free to operate out of his natural strength as a spiritual leader while unburdened by sole responsibility for others.

The story of Moses always serves as a reminder to me of the necessity for introverts like myself to claim solitude and "time out" on a regular basis. Introverted leaders, in particular, need to delegate responsibility in order to claim this time for themselves. Without opportunities for renewal, introverts become frustrated, overwhelmed, and ineffective, as Moses was in danger of becoming. When they claim the periodic solitude they need, introverts are able to express their natural gifts of spiritual and emotional depth. However, it is not only introverts who need solitude. Extroverts also need it, although for different reasons.

EXTROVERTS AND SOLITUDE

Since extroverts are drawn to people and events, they tend to live through these primary relationships, jobs, and roles in life. The danger is that extroverts have a tendency to lose themselves in their relationships and roles. Individuals with a strongly extroverted temperament and a highly developed sense of responsibility can, over a period of time, lose a sense of the core self in living out their responsibilities as parents, spouses, and breadwinners. These are all "good" responsibilities, but they can overwhelm us. An example of this loss of the self is Martha in the gospel story mentioned above: Martha is gently rebuked by Jesus for losing her sense of true priorities as a result of being overwhelmed by her household responsibilities. This is the danger for extroverts. Extroverts may not seek out solitude, as do introverts. But solitude, when it *is* experienced by extroverts, provides the opportunity to wrestle with the basic questions of life: Who am I? Where is my center? Where is my integrity? Who am I apart from my various roles in life? Psychiatrist Anthony Storr writes, "The extroverted person who tends to lose himself because of over-adaption to others may be able to recover, and express his true self in solitude."[3]

The fact is, introverts and extroverts express different patterns in regard to seeking solitude. Introverts usually know they need it and tend to seek it out. They possess an internal gyroscope, as it were, continually pointing them in the direction of solitude. Extroverts, on the other hand, also need solitude but for a different reason. They need it as a corrective to their strong outward orientation. Furthermore, extroverts tend not to be aware of their need for solitude and renewal and do not seek it out; they may even actively resist opportunities for it. The danger for extroverts, therefore, is that by ignoring their need for personal renewal they will tend to "choose" illness as a way of achieving a much-needed time out.

Introverts and extroverts also differ in the *amount* of solitude they require. Introverts require more solitude because they are easily drained of energy by their external involvements and need solitude to renew themselves. It is important to realize that this is a spiritual and psychological requirement for introverts—a direct consequence of their makeup.

Clinical psychologist Ester Schaler Buchholz writes, "Research suggests that to a degree the individual's need for aloneness may be 'hardwired' (that is, in our brain cells) before nurturing takes over."[4] If this is indeed the case, then the introvert's need for solitude is not an optional choice; rather, it is a requirement for effective functioning in the world.

The problem in our society for both introverts and extroverts is giving ourselves permission to claim necessary solitude and renewal on a regular basis. Giving ourselves permission begins with understanding and accepting who we are. Certainly there are potential dangers for both the introverted and extroverted temperaments. But there are also particular gifts that both offer by virtue of their different temperaments. Indeed, one could view an individual's natural temperament as one of the "gifts" that God has apportioned to each of us "for the common good" (1 Corinthians 12:7). If God has created each of us to be unique, presumably there is a reason for our differentness; there is a particular path, even a particular work, that God intends for each one of us for which we are uniquely suited. Seen in this way, our temperament, even with its inherent limitations, is not a "problem" to be resolved; it is instead God's gift to us and also points the way to a potential path for service.

Our need for solitude, however, depends not only upon our particular temperament. It depends also upon our stage of life. Indeed, our requirements for solitude change as we progress through life, as we shall see in the next chapter.

QUESTIONS FOR REFLECTION

1. Do you identify more strongly with Michael, extroverted and busy, or Carole, quietly contemplative? Which elements of each do you see in your own life?

2. Do you think temperamental differences are innate and not subject to change? Can you think of a time that you tried to "change" yourself? Did you succeed? Why or why not? What did you learn about yourself as a result?

3. The story of Mary and Martha can illustrate the strengths and weaknesses of two different temperaments. Do you see yourself as primarily a Mary or a Martha? What potential dangers of each have you noted in yourself? How have you learned to compensate?

4. In general, do you view your temperament as a problem to be overcome or as a potential path of service? If the latter, to which ministries do you think God may be leading you by means of your own particular temperament?

CHAPTER SIX

Solitude and the Life Cycle

A s we saw in the last chapter, our need for solitude depends in large part upon our temperament. There are individuals for whom solitude has
always been an important part of their everyday
lives. There are others for whom solitude is a sometimes thing, sought out on rare occasions. The need
for solitude, however, changes as we move through
life, from childhood and adolescence to young adulthood and midlife and, eventually, to old age.
Furthermore, our need for solitude always exists in
tension with the degree of solitude "permitted" by
the larger society and by our own particular life circumstances. In order to explore these changing

needs, let us look briefly at three individuals at different stages of life.

Sharon is a young mother in her late thirties whose life is filled with activity. She is constantly on the go with her three children, carpooling to various sports and school events and shepherding her two oldest children—who are as rushed and overcommitted as she is—through their crucial adolescent years. Sharon also works full time, both for her own self-satisfaction and also to maintain the family's comfortable upper-middle-class lifestyle. She is highly involved in her church, serving as chair of the worship committee. Sharon's life appears to be full and rich—and so indeed it is. But this fullness has been purchased at the cost of time for herself. Sharon wonders sometimes whether this constant round of activity has taken on a life—a dynamic—of its own. And she wonders whether the life she is living reflects the person she truly is. Sharon remembers one summer morning on a family vacation when she got up early and stole away from her husband and children for a solitary walk around the lake. Reveling in the early morning sounds of nature, she felt again in touch with aspects of herself buried under family, job, and social responsibilities. She wonders how she might incorporate more such interludes of solitude—however brief—into her busy life.

Adele is at the other end of the age spectrum. A woman in her mid-eighties, Adele was once as active and involved as Sharon. Those years are now, however, fifty years in the past. Age and physical infirmity have left her almost entirely homebound. The few friends who still remain are no longer mobile and able to visit her. Her two sons have moved out of the area, along with the grandchildren. If Sharon has little or no solitude, Adele has nothing but solitude. She lives alone with her memories, which are indeed a source of comfort, but her life lacks the necessary balance between solitude and involvement with others.

And then there is myself, the rector of Sharon's and Adele's church. At fifty-seven, I am situated in the life cycle somewhere between Sharon and Adele. Like Sharon, my life is extraordinarily busy, with professional commitments and family responsibilities taking up the bulk of my day: I, too, frequently "don't have a moment to myself." Unlike Sharon, however, I am coming to the end of the busy early adult/midlife period. In three or four years our children will be in college; in six or seven years, I will be retired.

In addition to these external changes, there are important internal changes for me as well. I sense in myself an increasing need for solitude and time for reflection. This was brought home a couple of years ago when we had a church consultant help the parish plan for the future. As part of a discernment process the consultant had us write an answer to the question, "What is the one thing you would change about your life?" I found myself writing, "I want *time*. I want time and space for myself." What surprised me was not *what* I had written, but the vehemence with which I had written it. I *really* wanted that time and space! Around this same time I had lunch with a colleague about my own age who said, "Since my mid-fifties I find myself becoming more reflective, more appreciative of solitude." Her words struck a chord of recognition in me.

These experiences of Sharon, Adele, and myself illustrate a basic fact about our need for solitude: it changes as we move through life. Our inner need for solitude changes as we grow older and more reflective. Furthermore, the amount and quality of solitude in our lives is shaped by social expectations and our own particular life circumstances. For young adults such as Sharon, as well as those approaching midlife, family responsibilities and professional commitments can make opportunities for solitude and reflection scarce. We often have a nagging feeling that the life we are living, as full and rich as it is, is not entirely our own.

Around midlife the ground begins to shift as external circumstances begin to change. Perhaps even more important, a strong internal agenda begins to assert itself, a need, in the words of Søren Kierkegaard, to find "a truth which is true for me." For individuals who have not been accustomed to reflection, such a period may be at first very unsettling. And then finally there are the latter years, during which external commitments and responsibilities begin to fall away and—ideally—we begin to take increased pleasure in our own company. This new phase has its own danger. We may discover that solitude is all we have.

Accepting and making sense of our changing requirements for solitude is made more difficult by the fact that society does not like to admit that we change spiritually as we get older. We deny aging by speaking of seniors as being so many years "young"

and we are entertained by Hollywood movies por-
traying male geriatrics as testosterone-addled
teenagers. Behind such portrayals is a denial of aging
and, ultimately, a denial of death. The fact is, not
only are our life tasks and circumstances different at
each age, *we* are different. As Carl Jung once stated,
"We cannot live the afternoon of life according to the
program of life's morning." To attempt to do so is to
do violence to our inner selves and to live without a
sense of authenticity.

Life circumstances and the requirements of life at
each particular stage exist in tension with the solitude we need, tending to deprive us of it during the
busy early adult and midlife years, and to overload
us with it during the latter years. In this chapter we
will examine our changing requirements for solitude
throughout the various stages of our lives.

CHILDHOOD AND ADOLESCENCE
We read the classics of children's literature of a previous era with a sense of amazement at the freedom
that children and adolescents enjoyed until relatively
recently. Today, Christopher Robin would be
enrolled in a day-care program instead of spending
his days in the woods with Pooh. Tom Sawyer would
be competing in travel soccer rather than wasting his
time down by the river with his friend Huck. One of
the striking phenomena of recent years is the almost
virtual disappearance of unstructured time for solitude in the lives of our children and adolescents. For
the most part, today's children and adolescents are
constantly *with* others in structured and supervised
activities.

This impression is well born out by the statistics. Children today spend eight hours a week more in school than they did two decades ago, are assigned more homework, and are fifty percent more likely to be involved in organized sports out of school. No wonder that children's leisure time—defined as time left over after sleeping, eating, personal hygiene, and attending school or day care, has decreased fifteen percent during the past two decades. An article in a national magazine profiles a typical overscheduled youngster:

> Steven Guzman is only 12, but he's booked solid. He wakes up at six every weekday morning, downs a five minute breakfast, reports to school at 7:50, returns home at 3:15, hits the books from 5 to 9 (with a break for dinner) and goes to sleep at 10:30. Saturdays are little better: from 9 to 5 he attends a prep program in the hope of getting a scholarship to a private school. Then there are piano lessons and a couple of hours of practice a week. If he's lucky, he'll squeeze in his friends on Sunday. "Sometimes I think, like, since I'm a kid, I need to enjoy my life," he says. "But I don't have time for that."[1]

There are many reasons for the disappearance of unstructured time alone in the lives of our children. Certainly parents' fears for the safety of their children is a major factor. So also is the increase in the number of households where both parents work outside the home and of single parent households. In addition, there is also a strong cultural bias against children having unstructured time alone. Whatever the reason, the disappearance of solitude and unstructured time alone has been purchased at a cost. A recent article on parenting states:

> The importance of quiet time is something that our culture fails to respect...thus we teach our children to fear silence and solitude—at the very least we distract them from it. In doing so, we also distract them from hearing their own inner voices and the Still Small Voice that's only heard in silence and solitude.[2]

We may well wonder what will be the impact of this lack of opportunity for solitude on the emotional and spiritual lives of children. Traditionally, children and adolescents have derived a sense of self from experiencing time alone and periodic withdrawal from their surroundings. In scripture we read the account of the twelve-year-old Jesus in the temple with the elders, having stolen away from his parents (Luke 2:41-52). This story is a kind of metaphor for the periodic withdrawal in which children and adolescents need to engage in order to become emotionally and spiritually mature adults. Are we raising a generation of children who, as adults, will be incapable of solitude, never having experienced it as children, and will therefore be out of touch with their inner lives? Or is the opposite true, that this generation will hunger for what they have been deprived of and will therefore seek it even more avidly as adults? Only time will tell.

ACTIVE ADULTHOOD

The adult years of the first half of life are by nature a time of intense involvement in social activities and in the wider community. These are the years of what the Hindu culture calls the "householder stage." It is during these years that most people forge a career or life work, establish ties of intimacy with others, marry, have children, and participate in the activities of social, religious, and civic institutions.

What is different about these years today, however, is that people are busy as never before. During the past generation or more, women have joined the workforce in large numbers, adding careers to their traditional roles as wife and mother. Men continue their traditional role as chief breadwinner, while sharing the responsibilities of parenthood and helping to maintain a household (not always equitably) with their overburdened, overcommitted, and overstressed spouses. In addition, with the rise in the divorce rate an increasing number of people are single parents, adding to the time demands placed upon them.

In addition to these easily documented societal changes, our use of leisure time has also changed within the past generation for young adults. As with their children, the change has been in the direction of increased involvement with others and away from opportunities for solitude and self-reflection. The focus on supervised children's activities has had a profound effect on parents' leisure time, especially that of mothers. According to a recent study, American women now spend fifteen percent more of their time driving on Saturday, doing errands and shuttling children to various activities, than they did during the early 1990s, while spending sixteen percent less time on hobbies and seventeen percent less time on reading, activities which traditionally provide individuals with opportunities for solitude.[3] Increasingly Americans engage in what authors John P. Robinson and Geoffrey Godbey call "hurried leisure": time that does not *feel* like leisure because one is continually rushing on to the next activity.[4] In general, young parents today share with their children the fact that they are overcommitted, overstressed, and deprived of opportunities for solitude and for personal renewal.

It is during these active adult years that the amount of solitude "permitted" by the larger society falls to an all-time low. One factor is the enormous time and energy required to fulfill the demands of our busy lives. Another is the social attitude that views time alone as selfish in that it takes time away from others. The result is that many active adults feel beleaguered, out of touch with themselves, and lacking time for spiritual or emotional growth.

MIDLIFE

At midlife the ground begins to shift beneath our feet. Dramatic external changes often occur. Children leave home, leaving an empty nest. Longtime troubled marriages end in divorce. Parents die, transforming midlifers into members of the "older generation." We peak in our careers, bringing to an end long-held and often unrealistic dreams. An unexpected illness reminds us of our own mortality. These external events trigger profound inner transformations and the need to come to terms with radically changed life circumstances. Consequently, solitude and the desire for solitude may begin to play a major role in our lives.

In addition to and sometimes separate from these life-altering external events are profound internal transformations, which may be all the more unsettling when there seems to be no external event to peg them on. We may experience a sense of disillusionment with our life and with what we have achieved. Such feelings leave us feeling lost and alone. It was approaching midlife that the poet Dante wrote in his *Divine Comedy* of finding himself "in a dark wood where the straight way was lost." In scripture, Ecclesiastes reflects the preoccupations of midlife, with its teaching that "all is vanity and a chasing after wind" (1:14). In the middle of his life Nicodemus comes to Jesus by night, inquiring how he who has "grown old" might be "born anew" (John 3:3, RSV).

There is a positive side to this crisis of meaning in midlife as well. Midlife is also the time when, in the words of Paul Tournier, "The *doing* and the *having* are giving way to the *being*."[5] Psychologist Roger Gould speaks of midlife, especially the years after fifty, as a time when "the life of inner-directedness finally prevails ... and this mysterious, indelible 'me' becomes our acknowledged core, around which we center the rest of our lives."[6]

This time of life in which the desire for solitude often plays a major role is well illustrated by two classic myths that dramatize the different and yet related paths men and women must take to achieve individuation, the fullest development of our unique selves, at midlife. The men's midlife myth is the story of Parsival and the Holy Grail, in which Parsival emerges from obscure upbringings in Wales to become the leading knight of King Arthur's kingdom. As he approaches midlife, however, Parsival becomes an increasingly hard, bitter, and disillusioned man. His outer life of conquest is now performed more out of a sense of habit than of inner conviction. Spiritually and psychologically, Parsival is at a dead end.

One day Parsival encounters a band of pilgrims and asks them where they are going. "To a hermit for Good Friday confession," they reply. With these words an important memory comes back to Parsival. He remembers the grail castle that he had discovered in the woods as an adolescent, an experience which had brought him into contact with the divine. At this moment it could be said of Parsival that he "came to himself," in the language of Jesus in the parable of the prodigal son. For the first time in years he is again in touch with a spiritual reality. The pilgrims invite him to join them as they make their way to the hut of the hermit, who turns out to be Parsival's uncle. The hermit, in other words, is part of Parsival himself, carrying his own genes, so to speak. When the hermit encounters Parsival he recites to him all of his faults and shortcomings over the years. However, he then gives him his benediction and tells Parsival he must go directly to the castle and claim for himself his spiritual heritage. The legend ends with Parsival posed to reclaim that healing spiritual quality inside himself which he had lost so many years before. Jungian analyst Robert Johnson writes of the figure of the hermit:

> The hermit is the introverted part of one's masculine heritage. One sees that the second million or the second wife or whatever extroverted activities he pursues isn't going to solve the problem.... This is the time for a man to take six weeks off from his job and go away to summon that hermit in himself, that extremely introverted sum of energy within him. This will give him the perspective he needs for the next stage of life.[7]

A contemporary example of the manner in which the grail myth is lived out in the life of a middle-aged man, and especially of the period of disillusionment that often precedes the spiritual awakening, is well described in a magazine article about a doctor who reassessed his life and professional activities at midlife. While in his forties Burt worked fifty to sixty hours every week and traveled on many weekends. He worked constantly but went home each day exhausted, with dozens of tasks left undone. Then when he turned fifty he took a year's sabbatical from his job, to allow time for him to decide whether to apply for the position of medical director. In the middle of his sabbatical year he decided to put his hat in the ring, but then, as one of the top six candidates, he withdrew his name several months later.

> "I knew I could take on the position only if I felt called to do it," he says. "I came to realize the job would be very business-oriented, which would not be in harmony with my values. I thought a lot about my values during my sabbatical. And

another one of my midlife issues was to stop taking responsibility for the whole and focus on
something smaller. At midlife, you need to decide
intentionally what needs to be done in the world
and what part of it you can do."[8]

Burt has since returned to medical practice three-
quarters time, leaving himself free for such new interests as gardening, pottery, and constructing a
meditation walk around the periphery of his urban
house.

As Parsival and the Holy Grail is the myth which
relates to men's midlife development, the female
equivalent is the Greek myth of Eros and Psyche.
This myth does not speak directly of the need to discover one's "inner hermit," but it does speak of a
kind of psychological distancing that women must
undertake at midlife in order for spiritual and personal growth to occur. And in this distancing, solitude—actual solitude—will often play a major role.

According to the story, Psyche, a princess in
Greek mythology and a child of mortals, has been
directed to descend to the underworld to retrieve a
jar of precious ointment in order to win back the
love of Eros, the Greek god of love. What makes this
task especially challenging is the fact that on the way
she must encounter and refuse to be distracted by
certain persons in need. The first is a lame donkey
driver, who will entreat her to help him pick up some
sticks. Next she will encounter a dying man, whose
hand reaches up from the depths of the river she
must cross. Finally she will encounter three women
who are weaving the Threads of Fate, who will ask
her assistance. All of these entreaties she is to ignore

as she descends into the underworld and obtains the jar of precious ointment. She is then to return back the same way, again refusing their entreaties, and continue on to complete her final task.

In its simplest terms, the myth of Eros and Psyche is saying to women, especially at midlife, that they must learn to refuse. Midlife is the time for women temporarily to curb their natural generosity of spirit, their "nurturing instinct," and to focus upon their own inner development. Once a woman has completed her own descent into the depths, into her own unconscious, if you will, and has integrated from it the insights that it alone can offer, then she can afford to be generous again, but now with a deeper sense of who she is and what her own special task is for the next stage of life.

The myth of Psyche speaks not only to women at midlife, but also to male and female nurturers at any stage of life. Clergy, social workers, counselors, medical personnel, teachers, and all those in nurturing professions need to focus their attention inward at midlife and to learn to say no to extraneous and unnecessary demands. In fulfilling this task, solitude will often play a major role.

THE LATTER YEARS

As we move into our latter years, solitude and a desire for solitude may play an increasingly important role. For those who have always valued time alone, opportunities for solitude in one's later years become even more precious. On the other hand, those who have avoided solitude and self-reflection may increasingly come to value these experiences.

They may discover the truth of the words written by psychologist Carl Jung in his essay on "The Stages of Life": "For the aging person it is a duty and a necessity to give serious attention to himself." Often the first experience of this change is during the period that author Tim Stafford calls the "second day" of old age, the time immediately following the first flush of retirement, when individuals feel an inner calling to sum up what they have achieved in life and to set new goals for the time remaining.[9]

As the *desire* for solitude increases in one's latter years, so also do the opportunities. Children are now long since grown and have left home. Retirement opens up new blocks of time to be used for creative purposes, including self-reflection. Author Margaret Guenther speaks of the second half of life as a time for "crafting"—expressing new gifts and interests and exploring our spiritual depths. Crafting takes time, notes Mary C. Morrison in her recent book on aging, and she describes why time is perhaps the most wonderful gift of old age:

> release from the everyday details and hassles of living that consume so much of middle age; plenty of "slow time," "hammock time," time to goof off, to do and be nothing, to experience the pleasure of waiting and patience to appreciate and be present in "the Eternal Now"; silence, solitude and serenity, and the chance to indulge "a good think" and inventory "the furniture of the soul."[10]

On the other side of the ledger, the latter years may bring entirely too much solitude. The death of a spouse, physical infirmity, and even retirement itself may plunge a person into loneliness and isolation. As the problem of the early and middle adult years may be too little solitude and too little time for oneself, so the problem of the latter years may be entirely too much. The book of Ecclesiastes urges its readers to "Remember your creator in the days of your youth, before the days of trouble come, and the years draw near when you will say, 'I have no pleasure in them.'" It speaks of old age as a time of diminished opportunity, when, for a variety of reasons, "the doors on the street are shut" (12:1, 4).

One for whom this was literally true was Margaret, a delightful widow in her eighties whom I used to visit on a regular basis. Margaret had lived for well over half a century in a working-class neighborhood outside Philadelphia. In recent years the neighborhood had deteriorated, however, and Margaret found herself a virtual prisoner in her home, afraid to venture outside or even to sit on her porch. The quiet streets where her children had played had become scenes of crime and violence. Margaret's adult children pleaded with her to move to a safer neighborhood, but the modest row house held memories and the prospect of moving seemed daunting to the elderly woman. After several years her children did persuade her to move to a senior citizen high-rise in a safer neighborhood, but until then age and changed circumstances had kept Margaret a prisoner behind closed doors.

Ultimately, of course, an increasing tendency toward solitude and even a psychological withdrawal from life can be viewed as a spiritual and psychological preparation for death. In this connection I think of my father's last years in a nursing home. Although in his late eighties, my father's mind was still sharp and his hearing unimpaired. He could easily have established relationships with the other residents of the nursing home had he wished. Instead he withdrew into a kind of self-imposed solitude. He would spend hours seated in his wheelchair in front of the French doors in the lobby, gazing out upon a small garden. I often wondered what he thought about during those long hours. I wanted to ask him but I was afraid of breaking in upon his great silence. Always an intensely private person, my father had taken upon himself the role of an anchorite in the context of a twentieth-century nursing home. When he died, I was reminded of the words of an obituary of another very quiet man, publisher Peter Fleishman, of whom it was written, "The quietness ended in silence."

In this chapter we have traced the differing needs for solitude at various stages of life, and how in solitude we can be guided into deeper levels of truth about ourselves. Ultimately, greater self-understanding leads to a deeper knowledge and awareness of God, a topic we will discuss in the next chapter.

QUESTIONS FOR REFLECTION

1. Has it been your experience that opportunities for solitude, and the need for it, change throughout life? Which periods of life have given you the most solitude? The least? Are you experiencing the right balance between solitude and involvement in your present stage of life?

2. Do you see a need for more opportunities for solitude in the lives of your children, or children you know? How could children be provided such opportunities while at the same time being protected from potential dangers?

3. Do you think men and women tend to seek solitude in different ways? How does this relate to your own experience? Describe some practical strategies you have worked out with a loved one to accommodate your differing needs for solitude.

4. Margaret Guenther has written that *crafting* your life is a task of the older years. How are you presently crafting your life? What, if any, is the part played by solitude?

CHAPTER SEVEN

Solitude and the Presence of God

There is a tiny spot of land off the northern coast
of England called St. Cuthbert's Isle. It is where
St. Cuthbert, one of the saints and mystics of the
early Christian church in Britain, retired to pray and
meditate. I discovered St. Cuthbert's Isle during the
summer of my second year of seminary, when I was
called to minister to a small congregation of fisher-
men and their families at Lindisfarne, a larger island
off the northern coast of Britain and one of the earliest centers of Christianity on the British Isles.
Cuthbert had been prior of the abbey at Lindisfarne
during the eighth century. It had been his custom
during his busy years of heading a monastic house to
pray and meditate on a tiny expanse of rock and

sand a couple of hundred feet off the coast of Lindisfarne. During high tide, when the island was cut off from Lindisfarne, Cuthbert was left completely alone to pray and meditate. During low tide a land bridge between the two islands gave access to a steady stream of villagers seeking Cuthbert's advice and counsel. Then high tide would return and Cuthbert would again be alone with his God.

The life of this early Christian saint, so unimaginably different from our lives in the twenty-first century, nevertheless speaks to me on several levels. It makes me aware of the need to alternate periods of solitude and of engagement, of reflection and involvement. Second, it affirms the strange relevance of the solitary individual who, like Cuthbert, brings forth the wisdom to help others live in the world. Finally, Cuthbert's life is a metaphor for those great "tides" of our lives, unrecognized and yet immutable, pulling us at one time toward involvement and engagement, at another time toward silence, solitude, and the presence of God.

To say that this chapter is about solitude and the presence of God is immediately to encounter a paradox: on the one hand our theology, to say nothing of our common sense, claims that God is present at all times and in all circumstances. On the other hand—and here we encounter the paradox—God seems to be present in a very special way in silence and solitude. I do not deny that we experience a sense of the presence of God in traditional corporate worship. I am suggesting, however, that even in such settings, at that moment when we feel closest to God, the corporate elements tend to recede, leaving us alone with God.

In her book *The Presence of Absence,* Doris Grumbach describes her powerful encounter with the divine in her late twenties. At the time she was a mother of two young children, living in a village north of New York City. Her husband took the children on an errand, and Grumbach relished her rare time alone.

> I do not remember thinking about anything in particular in that hour except perhaps how pleasant, in my noisy life, how agreeable, the silence was. What happened was this: sitting there, almost squatting on those wooden steps, listening to the quiet, I was filled with a unique feeling of peace, an impression so intense that it seemed to expand into ineffable joy, a huge delight....It went on, second after second, so pervasive that it seemed to fill my entire body. I relaxed into it, luxuriated in it. Then with no warning, and surely without preparation or expectation, I knew what it was: for the seconds it lasted I felt, with a certainty I cannot account for, a sense of the presence of God.[1]

This encounter with God in silence and solitude is certainly not unique. We have seen how the monastic tradition links the presence of God—or at least the perceived presence of God—with the experience of silence and solitude. Grumbach's experience as a young woman with no prior religious belief or training presents several paradoxes. In the church we teach the importance of spiritual formation and following traditional religious practices, such as prayer, Bible reading, and worship, and sharing the fellowship of believers. And yet Grumbach's experience demonstrates that the opposite can also be true: people can feel God's presence without prior religious training, outside the community of faith, and, indeed, without even expecting such an experience. We are left with the conclusion that God is far less predictable than we sometimes think, and that Jesus was stating a profound spiritual truth when he said to Nicodemus, "The wind [the Spirit of God] blows where it chooses" (John 3:8). Above all, we are reminded of the importance of silence and solitude in apprehending the presence of God.

And so we return then to the dilemma with which we began this chapter. If indeed it is true that God is present in all places and all circumstances, why is it that God's presence can often be perceived more clearly in silence and in solitude? Perhaps an analogy would be helpful. Scientists tell us that radio waves are constantly in the air, capable at any moment of being transmitted. What these radio waves require in order to be heard is a clear signal, that is, an absence of static. In a similar fashion we too need an absence of "static" in order to feel the presence of God and hear God's "still, small voice."

The problem is that we live in a world of static— "static" in the form of social expectations placed upon us, the responsibilities for others laid upon us, and our own fears, hopes, and dreams. It requires a degree of silence and solitude—and not only in a literal but also a metaphorical sense—to allow this "static" to clear so that we can feel the presence of God and hear God's voice within us. Knowing this, and perhaps actually having experienced such "static-free" zones in our own past, we might resolve intentionally to seek out silence and solitude from time to time. In order to do this, however, we need first to confront our own powerful resistance to silence and solitude—a resistance caused in part, ironically enough, by the community of faith itself.

SOLITUDE IN THE FAITH COMMUNITY

Solitude is often perceived by the church as a form of escapism, a way of avoiding personal and social involvement. The faith community tends to perceive solitude as a form of pietism, an escape from the problems of the world, and contrasts it to an involved and committed social activism. But the fact is, in scripture solitude is seen not as a means of escape but as an arena for struggle. We seek in vain for examples of individuals, like Jacob, Elijah, and Jesus himself, who seek solitude to obtain "peace of mind" in a modern sense; instead, we encounter individuals who experience solitude as a stage for battle. Solitude in scripture is far from peaceful: it is a place where we come to battle for our soul. In fact, from the Bible's point of view, we could reverse our society's assumptions about solitude: solitude is not a place we go to *avoid* our problems; it is, rather, the avoidance of solitude that is the escape. Indeed, the individual who has the courage to choose solitude better be prepared for battle!

So it is in our own lives. Initially we may experience solitude as a relief, especially if coming upon the heels of an overly busy and conflicted period in our lives. At such times we may very well experience something of the "peace of mind" that is our society's stereotype for solitude. After that, however, the real battle for personal and spiritual transformation begins. As one author writes of Thomas Merton's decision to embrace a life of solitude: "He experienced all that comes with such a decision—fear and angst—the specter of self-centeredness, and the difficulty of balancing contemplation with society."[2] Such a struggle leads to a kind of death. But it is a death that leads to a resurrected sense of who we really are, and of our relation to God.

Our society's other great misconception about solitude is that it constitutes an attempt to disengage from life. Again, solitude *can* lead to disengagement and in fact disengagement may be our initial motivation in seeking solitude, especially after a period of conflict or trauma in our lives. However, the assumption that solitude leads to a permanent withdrawal from life is simply not born out by scripture or by the example of men and women who have experienced solitude and who have emerged to become more engaged—not less—in life. The modern view of solitude as an escape into irrelevance and away from responsibility is simply not born out by the biblical narrative. Instead, solitude is the necessary first step in creative engagement with the world. Indeed, it is likely that *without* this radical disengagement, it may not be possible to live with the depth, intensity, and commitment to which God is calling each of us on our separate paths.

For those who feel drawn to solitude, especially at certain periods of their lives, and who may be concerned about escapism, it is important to realize that solitude *is* indeed a necessary first step in reengagement. That does not mean a need for solitude is a call to a whole new lifestyle that will shut out the world. Indeed, following a period of personal crisis or transition, one may never again experience such an intense need for solitude. The fruits of a period of retreat may simply be incorporated into one's life and revisited from time to time. Jesus, for example, apparently never again experienced the depth, intensity, and duration of his original wilderness experience or, if he did, it is not recorded in scripture. But after his forty days in the wilderness, solitude remained for Jesus a deep pool from which he was able to draw when he was faced with crucial decisions about his ministry, or simply needed to commune with his Father in a "lonely place."

This need for intense solitude at a crucial point of decision-making in one's life can be seen in the experience of a New York stockbroker who was living the ambitious professional life she had always desired. In her late twenties, however, Mary began to feel that a life devoted only to making money for her clients would not ultimately satisfy her. Taking a one-year sabbatical, she left New York to work as a maid in the inn at Yellowstone National Park. As the busy summer gave way to the quieter autumn and winter and the crowds departed, Mary had time to ponder where God might be leading her. The climax of the year came on New Year's Eve, when she made a midnight pilgrimage to Old Faithful Geyser. Here where thousands gather every summer, on the one night of the year when millions congregate with family and friends, Mary was alone, watching Old Faithful erupt in the silence of the night. The impact of that

experience was not immediately felt: at the end of the
year Mary returned to her work as a stockbroker.
But two years later Mary acted on the decision she
had pondered that night, and entered seminary to
become an Episcopal priest.

SOLITUDE IN WORSHIP

If solitude is a state in which God is encountered in
a special way as well as a necessary first step in reen-
gaging in the world, what then should be the attitude
of the faith community toward solitude? Let us take
this a little further and ask: How could the church
actually *help* and *encourage* individuals in experiencing their own solitude?

The first step would be simply to give permission.
So often the church discourages those who would
seek a more solitary path. Statements such as, "There
is no such thing as a solitary Christian," while true
enough on a certain level, nevertheless have the effect
of instilling a sense of guilt in those who are drawn
to solitude. The community of faith needs to recognize that its emphasis on group participation is not
entirely altruistic and contains an element of self-
interest. Warnings against pursuing a solitary path
often are motivated far more by the need for institutional survival and a fear that individuals will begin
to worship the god of the golf course than they are
by a concern about real spiritual dangers. Rather
than denigrating the concept of solitude, the community of faith needs to affirm the solitary path as
one valid expression of an individual's total spiritual
journey, and to recognize that solitude and participa-

tion in the life of a congregation can be complementary expressions of a life of faith.

Second, the community of faith, and the local church in particular, could make available to their members a designated "holy space" for experiencing silence and solitude. Such a holy space could be as simple as a furnished room in a parish hall that someone could reserve for a few hours or a whole day. If a church is fortunate enough to have available to it a furnished house or apartment, such a place could be offered to members as an overnight retreat spot. It could also be made available to members of neighboring churches in order to share the expense of maintaining such a space. At the very least, a church could designate a chapel or meditation room as a place for private devotions. Such retreat spaces could be modeled on the idea of the *poustinia* of the Russian Orthodox tradition—a free-standing chapel available for individual prayer and reflection. Whatever form it takes, such a holy space could function as a "desert spot" in which individuals could engage their own wilderness, find solace and, if need be, struggle with the hard issues of their lives.

Churches can also make a greater effort to sponsor retreats in which parishioners can experience a measure of silence and solitude. The typical church retreat, mirroring our culture, tends to be oriented toward doing tasks and enjoying fellowship. Vestry retreats, for example, are usually focused on "getting to know one another" and identifying goals for the future and tasks to be accomplished. The typical parish retreat tends to place great emphasis on "building fellowship" and is oriented toward group process and facilitating interaction among participants. What is often missing from parish life is a contemplative, meditative retreat structured to allow individuals to claim silence and solitude for themselves. Such a retreat would have content and focus, but it would also incorporate large blocks of time for prayer and reflection. A brief morning and afternoon meditation would be followed by free time for prayer, reading, and reflection, and perhaps a walk around the grounds. Often the most important "work" of the retreat takes place during those times apart. Such a retreat would provide a valuable service for church members who cannot give themselves "permission" to claim silence and solitude for themselves in the midst of their daily lives by providing an opportunity for them to do so in church, if only for a few hours or a weekend.

The church could also make greater use of its rich resources of liturgy to incorporate the virtues of silence and solitude. One of my most unforgettable worship experiences occurred in a small New England Congregational church many years ago. In place of formal intercessions, the minister simply invited members of the congregation to sit comfortably (not stand or kneel, as is the Episcopal custom), to relax their breathing, to shut their eyes, and to focus on the prayers. No congregational response to the prayers was required; thus the individual's concentration was not broken by the need to make the proper response at the proper time. At the end of this seven or eight minutes of reflective prayer, I emerged spiritually and emotionally refreshed in a way that I have not experienced since. I have often thought that the Prayers of the People in the Episcopal Church could be offered in a similar reflective, meditative manner. This style would work especially well in a small mid-week service but it could also be incorporated into a larger celebration if the congregation were adequately prepared.

The fact is, the 1979 *Book of Common Prayer* incorporates silence to a much greater degree than previous prayer books have. Silence is directed after the lessons and immediately before significant acts, such as the words of ordination. Two of the forms for the Prayers of the People provide for moments of silence, as does the Penitential Order prior to the confession of sins. And yet in practice these rubrics are often observed perfunctorily or not at all. Rather than ignoring these rubrics, the church could even expand upon them, in order to incorporate silence and a kind of inner solitude into the context of corporate worship. The introduction of silence into worship, however, should not be attempted without careful preparation, including an explanation of the uses of silence in worship.

KEEPING THE SABBATH

Perhaps one of the most important ways we could introduce more silence and solitude into our lives would be to rediscover the real significance of keeping the sabbath. In our pluralistic culture the emphasis would have to be placed not on the sabbath as a particular day of the week, but rather as an important principal to be integrated into our lives. The concept of keeping the sabbath does not speak specifically to the concept of solitude, but it does underline the importance of creating a kind of spiritual and psychological "space" in which solitude may play a part.

The irony is that today we think of the fourth commandment, "Remember the sabbath day, and keep it holy," as the most expendable. Those who would not think of committing murder, adultery, or stealing think nothing of routinely breaking the fourth commandment, which was originally considered one of the most important. In both its versions (Exodus 20:8-11 and Deuteronomy 5:12-15), more words are devoted to this commandment than to any other. The sabbath is mentioned in all the great ethical codes in the first five books of the Old Testament, and violations of it were punishable by death (Exodus 31:15).

As we miss the importance attached to the fourth commandment today, so we also routinely misunderstand the real significance of it. We typically think of "keeping the sabbath" as attending worship. In fact, when we actually read the words of this commandment we discover that not one word is said about worship; rather, it commands a day of absolute rest:

> Observe the sabbath day and keep it holy, as the LORD your God commanded you. Six days you shall labor and do all your work. But the seventh day is a sabbath to the LORD your God; you shall not do any work—you, or your son or your daughter, or your male or female slave, or your ox or your donkey, or any of your livestock, or the resident alien in your towns, so that your male and female slave may rest as well as you. (Deuteronomy 5:12-14)

The Hebrew sabbath was intended to be, and was apparently indeed experienced, not as a burden but rather as a day of renewal and refreshment. The sabbath was a day of private prayer and meditation as well as public worship, a time to return to one's spiritual roots. One can imagine that in the quiet times alone as well as in the community observances, many experienced a "solitude of the heart," a feeling that they were alone in the presence of God. The assumption standing behind the Hebrew sabbath, and indeed behind Jesus' retreats to a "lonely place," was not necessarily that God was more *present* in silence and solitude. It was rather that a periodic reduction of distractions tends to make God more accessible to us so we can hear God's voice more clearly.

This emphasis on spiritual and psychological renewal makes the concept of the sabbath decidedly relevant to us today. Americans in particular live constantly "under the gun" in their work and even in their leisure. A joke at one of the Fortune 500 companies with a notoriously workaholic culture is, "If you don't come to work on Saturday, don't bother coming back on Sunday." The concept of the sabbath reminds us that we need a break periodically from the sense of urgency that dominates most of our lives. The sabbath reminds us that we need a break not only from paid work but also from work disguised as leisure. And it even suggests to us that perhaps, from time to time, we need a break from people as well, a "sabbath" from the constant interactions with others, so we may again experience silence and solitude as a path to God.

QUESTIONS FOR REFLECTION

1. Have you ever experienced God's presence in solitude? What were the circumstances? How were you subsequently able to integrate the fruits of this experience into your life and faith?

2. Do you see solitude as an escape from the problems of the world or an opportunity to wrestle with them? Recollect a time when you struggled with a personal crisis in solitude. What were the qualities of solitude that enabled you to resolve your problem?

3. Often there is a tension between solitude and involvement with others in a faith community. Do you believe both are necessary for spiritual growth? How might how your church incorporate silence and solitude into its worship and ongoing life as a faith community?

4. How did you respond to the suggestion that people need to incorporate elements of the traditional sabbath into their lives? Which such elements could you incorporate into your own life? How would you begin?

CHAPTER EIGHT

Reclaiming Solitude

I have had a recurring dream for many years in which I find myself in a small village. It is a terribly *busy* village with people rushing about. I am very much a part of all this busy activity, but I sense also that it is becoming oppressive for me. I need something else but I am not sure what it is. At this point my gaze wanders up to the roofs of the village houses and suddenly I see huge mountains towering outside the village. I am awestruck by their immensity and their silence. *That* is where I need to be, I say to myself. *That* is where I need to go. At this point my eyes fall on the village clock. I see that it is already a quarter to four. It is too late to go, I say to myself. By the time I get up into the mountain it will already be dark. Tomorrow I will go. Tomorrow I will get up into the mountains and have a full day in the silence and the solitude. At this point the dream always ends.

I have come to think of this dream as symbolic of both my own need for solitude and that of many people in our society. We all live in this busy village from which something else calls us. We all sense, each in our own way, those great looming peaks outside the village. But then we look at the clock. Tomorrow, we say to ourselves. Tomorrow we will get away. Tomorrow we will give ourselves the time and space we need.

A recent visit to a bookstore confirms this call many of us have to solitude. On display are calendars for the year to come, and many of them feature places of majestic beauty and profound solitude: mountain vistas, scenes from the Grand Canyon or the ocean, a solitary figure kayaking on a river. Prominent among them is a New England lighthouse calendar, a different lighthouse featured for each month of the year. What is the appeal of this way of life that has no practical relevance to virtually any American today? Is it not because the lighthouse, and the image of the solitary lighthouse keeper, speaks to something deep inside us?

The tension between attachment and detachment, between involvement and withdrawal, is hardly unique to our times. We remember the gospel incident in which Jesus withdraws to the hills to pray, only to be pursued by the crowds. What is perhaps new, however, and to some extent unique, is the multiplicity of the demands placed upon us, coupled with the lack of any recognition on the part of the larger society that occasional withdrawal and periods of solitude can be beneficial. Many individuals seek some way of routinely integrating solitude and renewal into their busy lives, but are not quite sure how to go about it. It is the purpose of this chapter to discuss how to claim that needed solitude and renewal and also what we might actually do with it once we have it.

GIVING OURSELVES PERMISSION

There is a poignant scene at the end of A. A. Milne's children's classic, *The House at Pooh Corner*. Christopher Robin is preparing to go to school, and is saying goodbye to his beloved friend and goodbye to his childhood:

> Then, suddenly again, Christopher Robin, who was still looking at the world, with his chin in his hands, called out "Pooh!"
> "Yes?" said Pooh.
> "When I'm—when—Pooh!"
> "Yes, Christopher Robin?"
> "I'm not going to do nothing any more."
> "Never again?"
> "Well, not so much. They don't let you."
> Pooh waited for him to go on, but he was silent.[1]

Like Christopher Robin, as we grow to adulthood, society withdraws permission to "do nothing." The process begins in childhood, and by our teens and early twenties it is virtually complete. We are taught to be productive and, above all, to avoid solitude. Author Jessamyn West has written:

The prohibition against solitude is forever. A Carry Nation rises in every person when he thinks he sees someone sneaking off to be alone. It is not easy to be solitary unless you are also born ruthless. Every solitary repudiates someone.[2]

My own claiming of permission for solitude occurred at midlife. I found myself tired of constantly running, constantly responding to everyone's demands. I was weary of responding to those voices inside me continually flogging me on to more soul-deadening activity and involvements. One day I decided to take action in a small but significant way by setting aside every Thursday morning for quiet reading and reflection at home. This was not to be a time to take care of "practical" affairs, but for reflection and for work of a more creative nature. Even after I had set aside this half-day, however, I kept finding other things to do. I would tell myself, "Things are really piling up at work. I need to use just this Thursday alone to get to the mail." Or it would be the monthly church newsletter. Or even preparing my income tax return. Or I would find some excuse to go to the church office. Finally, after about a year of on-again, off-again use of my Thursday at-home time, I came to the realization that there will *always* be mail. There will always be the newsletter. There always be practical concerns.

I began to see the enormous wisdom and insight in the biblical account in Exodus of the escape of the Hebrew people from bondage in Egypt. Moses goes to Pharaoh to get permission for the people to leave, and over and over again Pharaoh refuses. Even after he finally does give permission, he subsequently withdraws it and instead pursues the Hebrew people into the wilderness. If we, like the Hebrew people, wait for complete "permission" to claim the solitude and renewal we need, we may wait forever. At some point we must do what the Hebrew people did: they left "in haste." In other words, they simply claimed their freedom and moved on.

However, the issue of permission brings up an important question. How can we make others our allies in claiming solitude, rather than the controlling Pharaoh who always says no? Marsha Sinetar, in her book *Ordinary People as Monks and Mystics,* gives examples of the various innovative ways that married people can address individual needs for solitude and privacy.[3] Some couples take advantage of work schedules that keep them apart during a portion of the week. Others take advantage of a vacation house for periodic retreats. Still others simply spend time apart from each other in separate portions of the house. Parents can arrange to leave their children periodically with a neighbor, friend, or their own parents.

PREPARING FOR SOLITUDE

When practical arrangements have been made and when you have alerted your loved ones of your need for occasional solitude, then you must prepare yourself to make optimal use of it. The first step is to *simplify.* This means clearing your calendar for an hour, an afternoon, or a long weekend. On a deeper level it means challenging the very assumptions that have led you to become overburdened and overwhelmed. This is not an easy task, as you are challenging our society's view of a "successful" person as one who never has time for him or herself. Henri Nouwen describes the ambiguity many feel by recounting his own emotions after living seven months in a Trappist monastery:

> I realized that I was caught in a web of strange paradoxes. While complaining about too many demands, I felt uneasy when none were made. While speaking about the burden of letter writing, an empty mailbox made me sad. While fretting about tiring lecture tours, I felt disappointed when there were no invitations. While speaking nostalgically about an empty desk, I feared the day on which that would come true. In short: while desiring to be alone, I was frightened of being left alone. The more I became aware of these paradoxes, the more I started to see how much I had indeed fallen in love with my own compulsions and illusions.[4]

Confronting our compulsions and illusions, as Nouwen calls them, is a necessary first step in claiming solitude. Otherwise, solitude will simply be one more thing to "do" in an otherwise overburdened, overstressed life.

The second step is to *identify* clearly exactly what it is we are seeking in our solitude. Obviously the purpose will differ from one person to another. In general, however, what we may be seeking at first is a "time out," a rest for overstressed and overloaded minds and bodies. Beyond this, however, is a deeper purpose of which we may at first not even be aware, and that is to relate to God and to our deeper self. We wish to hear God's voice speaking inside us. But as we remember from the story of Elijah, that "still, small voice" can be easily drowned out by the clamor of the world and by our own conflicting emotions. Hearing this voice, however, is the necessary first step in renewing contact with God and with ourselves.

Third, we should prepare to enter solitude in an attitude of what the desert fathers called *watchfulness*. As the writer of *The Philokalia* states, "This is not simple silence, but an attitude of listening to God and of openness to Him." It is this quality that the Benedictines call mindfulness. Developing this quality takes practice. We begin by deliberately slowing our actions. Pretend you are doing everything in slow motion. As you do so, notice your environment. Look at how the sun shines on the wall. Become aware of the ticking of the clock, or the sound of the wind. Notice the movement of your body through space. Between activities, sit quietly and hear the "sounds of silence."

Fourth, realize that achieving the benefits of solitude takes *time*. In achieving the benefits of solitude, as in parenting, there is no such thing as "quality time" as a substitute for real time. The benefits of solitude cannot be rushed. One of the most dramatic examples of the fact that achieving the benefits of solitude takes time is that of explorer Admiral Richard Byrd's experience in Antarctica during the winter of 1934. Byrd spent five and a half months in complete isolation manning an advance weather station on the southern continent. Byrd's reason for undertaking this grueling experience was largely personal. He wrote:

> I wanted something more than just privacy in the geographical sense. I wanted to sink roots into some replenishing philosophy.... I should have time to catch up, to study and think and listen.

His hopes for solitude were realized. On May 25, 1934, he wrote in his journal:

> Solitude is greater than I anticipated. My sense of values is changing.... I am better able to tell what in the world is wheat for me and what is chaff.[5]

What is fascinating about Byrd's experience, however, is that this breakthrough did not occur until the sixty-fourth day of his solitude. Do not be concerned if at first your own time of solitude seems unproductive. Have patience with your solitude and with yourself, and the benefits of solitude will reveal themselves.

WHAT DO WE DO IN SOLITUDE?

Once we have actually "claimed" the time for solitude we need, what do we actually *do* in solitude? What are the personal activities and spiritual practices that make for a "good solitude," one that brings us into deeper contact with God and with ourselves?

When you first enter the solitude, whether for an afternoon, a weekend, or longer, the best plan at first is no plan. Let the Holy Spirit lead you. You may want simply to sit quietly, to let the stillness gather about you, or to take long walks on the beach or on wooded trails. Give yourself permission to do nothing. There is a delightful story about an individual who comes upon another sitting quietly. "Are you sitting and thinking?" the first persons asks. "No, just sitting," the second replies. There is a time for just sitting, for not being "productive." During these early stages of solitude, whole hours or even days may be spent simply sitting quietly, reading, praying, walking, performing simple chores, exploring your new environment, and, in general, letting the Holy Spirit lead you.

After you have spent some time in such an enjoyable, gentle manner, you may find that some routine is naturally beginning to evolve. Exactly what this routine will be will naturally depend upon your preferences and interests. However, it will probably include some combination of the following elements, which many have found helpful in achieving a good solitude.

Reading and reflection. The monks of the Middle Ages called it *lectio divina,* or "holy reading," a reading of the scriptures with one's heart, focused less upon rational understanding than upon an openness and receptivity to the images of scripture. In our own solitude, we might enlarge upon the concept of *lectio* to include not only the scriptures but also any reading that speaks to our soul. This could be anything from the *Chicken Soup* books to the classics of the spiritual and devotional life. For those who enjoy crafts or art, recognizing that God often speaks through the work of our hands, *lectio* could perhaps even include a book on woodworking or oil painting. I personally find that *lectio* works best for me when I read relatively little and stop frequently to reflect on what I am reading.

Journaling. Related to holy reading is "holy writing," or journaling. A spiritual journal is different from a diary in that, instead of recording outward events, you document your inner life, your hopes and dreams, your worries and concerns. Journaling is an especially valuable technique in attempting to work through a particular question. If your intention is personal clarification or insight, you can use your journal to "name your fear," conversing with yourself and exploring several sides of an issue. Journaling is a verbal way of wrestling with a dilemma, as Jacob wrestled with God. Like Jacob, we may win a blessing and perhaps even, symbolically, a new name.

Physical activity. Exercise and mindful physical labor can play an important role in creative solitude. The monks of the Middle Ages believed that *labor manuum,* or manual labor, was an important part of the spiritual life, and the Benedictines' motto was *ora et labora,* prayer and work. Intense physical activity may be the way to a healing of the spirit, leaving us renewed and emotionally rejuvenated. After the death of his wife, psychologist Carl Jung poured much of his creative energy into fashioning stone sculptures. Late in life he wrote, "Everything that I have written this year and last year...has grown out of the stone sculptures I did after my wife's death."⁶

Prayer. Prayer is the traditional means of relating to God and, in so doing, giving voice to our own hopes, dreams, and fears. There are many different forms of prayer that speak to particular personality types and temperaments.[7] You may find yourself attracted to Franciscan prayer, expressing joy in the beauty of God's creation. Or you may be more drawn to the intellectual rigor of the Thomistic approach, achieving spiritual growth through logical, rational thinking. Whatever form of prayer you personally find most congenial, it is important to remember that prayer is listening as well as talking. As in any relationship, we have to hear what our partner is saying before we respond. So also in our relationship with God. You may find that it is easier to listen when you are doing something else. God often reveals himself in new and startling ways when we are involved in some simple task.

When we first enter into solitude, our prayer life may be very informal and rudimentary. Later we may feel the need to be somewhat more intentional. Members of the monastic orders built their days around the *opus dei,* or "liturgy of the hours," praising God at regular, specified intervals during the day and night. In time we too may feel a need to set aside certain times for prayer. Early morning after we get up, at noon, and at night before we go to bed are especially good times for prayer.

Finally, it is important not to become discouraged if our prayer life seems unproductive or even sterile at first. Scripture reminds us that when "we do not know how to pray," the Holy Spirit "intercedes with sighs too deep for words" (Romans 8:26). Indeed, at times of personal distress and conflict, sighing may be the only form of prayer of which we are capable.

Dreaming and daydreaming. Another invaluable technique for spiritual growth and self-discovery, especially during periods of solitude, is recording and interpreting our dreams. Looking to dreams for spiritual and emotional insight has long been a spiritual tradition, as reflected in scripture. The ancient Greek custom of dream incubation, in which an individual sought guidance while sleeping in the temple of Asklepios, the god of healing, may have ancient echoes in the Old Testament account of Eli and the boy Samuel sleeping in the temple (1 Samuel 3:1-10). Dreams are similar to the parables of Jesus in that the meaning is not always immediately clear. At other times and on other occasions, however, dreams can be startling in their clarity, especially at times of major life transition. Dream insights are all the more powerful in that they originate from a source outside the conscious self. Even if you do not immediately understand the significance of a particular dream, write it down. The meaning may gradually reveal itself as you subsequently reflect upon it.

Solitude is also a time for daydreaming. We were taught as children that daydreaming is a waste of time. In reality, daydreams—especially those that recur repeatedly—may point to hopes and dreams that we have kept buried. Solitude is a good time not only for daydreaming but also for asking whether certain persistently recurring and emotionally charged daydreams may in fact be God's way of pointing us to new directions.

Playfulness. Solitude is also a time for expressing an often overlooked quality of life, especially for adults, which is playfulness, or what author

Margaret Guenther in her book *Toward Holy Ground* calls "holy uselessness." What better opportunity to be playful than in solitude, with no one looking disparagingly over your shoulder? I am struck by how often in scripture God and the created world are portrayed as playful in nature. The book of Job describes the cosmic jubilee at the creation of the world, "when the morning stars sang together and all the heavenly beings shouted for joy" (Job 38:7). The psalms are full of playful images, from the mountains that "skipped like rams" (Psalm 114:4) to God's creation of the oceans and the Leviathan, the great sea monster "that you formed to sport in it" (Psalm 104:26). If God can create a world filled with singing stars, skipping mountains, and a sea monster whose express purpose is to play in the ocean, then surely we are justified in expressing our human pleasure in joy, creativity, and playfulness.

When I was writing this book, I took a week in Maine one February for research and writing. One bright, sunny day during that week I had a strong desire to go sledding with my dog on the golf course. "I can't go sledding," I said to myself. "I have a book to write. Besides, I'm fifty-seven years old." Fortunately, another voice inside me said, "Of course you can go sledding. If you go sledding you will be able to concentrate much better on the book. Besides, what does being fifty-seven have to do with it?" The result of this was that my dog and I spent an exhilarating afternoon sledding on the golf course, the dog joyfully chasing my sled down the hill on the sixth fairway. Expressing my playfulness not only rejuvenated and refreshed me; it also helped me concentrate better on the book, as my inner voice promised me it would.

Before leaving the topic of what we do in solitude, it may be helpful to note what appear to be some gender differences between men and women, both in their willingness to claim solitude as well as in what they choose to do in their solitude. Ester Schaler Buchholz, in her book *The Call of Solitude,* suggests that women often experience more ambivalence than men in claiming solitude. Men typically act on such desires by means of traditional male activities, such as hunting, fishing, camping, sailing, and woodworking, or simply going off on an extended business trip. Women, on the other hand, while experiencing an equivalent desire for "space," nevertheless resist the separation that acting on it involves. As a result, men are often more successful than women in claiming solitude for themselves.

As men and women differ in their willingness to claim solitude, so they also appear to differ in the nature of the activities they pursue. Men's solitude typically has an activist quality. While researching this book, I was struck by how often men, when undergoing a spiritual or emotional crisis, would go off into the wilderness or would engage in heavy construction. Bill Henderson wrote a book called *Tower: Faith, Vertigo, and Amateur Construction* about the spiritual and emotional healing he experienced building a tower in the woods and the examples of notable men—including Jung and Yeats—who also built towers. Women in crisis, on the other hand, would write about pulling up stakes, settling in a new environment, and gradually building a new network of relationships. In this connection it is fascinating that, whereas the root meaning of the word for both monk and monastery, *mono,* means "alone" or "single," the root word for convent, *convenire,* means "to meet together."[8] It may be that the scriptural paradigm for men seeking solitude is found in the accounts of Elijah, Paul, and indeed of Jesus himself, who all sought solitude in the wilderness, whereas the scriptural paradigm for women appears to be more that of Mary in the Mary and Martha story, who claimed her own solitude amid a network of family and friends. If we can manage to see beyond the potential stereotyping in these examples of perceived gender differences, they may point in a helpful fashion to the different and creative ways that men and women make use of solitude.

In conclusion, as we begin to incorporate solitude into our lives, we will find ourselves drawn to one or more of these traditional or nontraditional ways. We will find what "works" for us, and a routine, a "rule," if you will, will begin to emerge. I suspect that this was true as well of the desert fathers and of the monastic communities that grew out of their experience. What evolved into their rule was an incorporation of the practices that worked for them, that brought them closer to God and that spoke to their own human needs for meaning, for self-insight, and for the productive use of mind and body. A similar pattern of activities and practices will also evolve for us as we begin to reclaim solitude.

AFTER SOLITUDE, THEN WHAT?

After you reclaim solitude and begin to experience the benefits of it, how can you continue to incorporate it into your life and make sure that you do not lose the benefits you have gained? First, you might consider establishing your own "rule of life." My own rule, informal as it is, started some thirty years ago when I discovered that my early morning time, right after I got up, was a particularly good time to record dreams that seemed to have a meaning or significance for me. From this evolved an early morning pattern of reading, reflection, and writing. Gradually other elements also evolved: an early morning walk with the dog, one morning a week working at home, and, every season, a day-long excursion to a favorite hiking spot. My "rule," as I say, is quite informal. And yet I find that when it is broken—when, for example, I use my early morning time for practical matters—I find myself out-of-sorts and unfocused for the rest of the day. I keep my "rule" not because it *is* a rule but simply because it works for me. It helps me incorporate a measure of solitude and silence into my busy life.

Related to keeping a rule is maintaining the balance between attachment and detachment, between activity and reflection. It is probably fair to say that, without an intentional focus on maintaining such a balance, most of us will end up out of balance most of the time. The warning from Proverbs that "a false balance is an abomination to the LORD" (11:1) can be applied to the task of maintaining the balance between involvement and detachment, as it was to its original context of weights and measures. The fact is, most of us are too heavily weighted on the side of attachment. Necessary periods of self-reflective "space" are largely missing. It is good to remind ourselves that what we are seeking to "claim" when we seek solitude is not an unworldly lifestyle as an alternative to our own but rather a *balanced* lifestyle, one in which the inner and the outer are in creative harmony.

How do we maintain such a balance in the face of constant intrusions? The answer is, we do what Jesus did: we keep working at it. There were times that Jesus withdrew to a "deserted place" to pray but was pursued by his disciples and the crowds. At such times Jesus responded to the human needs of the moment, telling the disciples, "Let us go on to the neighboring towns, so that I may proclaim the message there also; for that is what I came out to do" (Mark 1:38). But afterward Jesus inevitably returned to the prayerful silence and solitude that renewed him.

When you begin to reclaim solitude, you will find that your inner life will intensify. Questions, concerns, and issues that have heretofore been buried will come to the surface. For this reason it is good to consider working with a spiritual director. A spiritual director is similar to a counselor or psychotherapist in that you meet with this person on a regular basis for guidance and direction. Unlike a psychotherapist, however, a spiritual director works out of the Christian tradition and looks to the Holy Spirit as the ultimate guide. The goal of spiritual direction is not adjustment to society but rather growth in your spiritual life. To find a competent and qualified spiritual director, contact your church, denominational office, a nearby convent or monastery, or speak to someone of your acquaintance who has recently undergone spiritual direction.

Finally, if you experience solitude as a familiar rhythm, you will gradually strengthen your ability to experience a solitude of the heart regardless of your external circumstances. Even in the midst of active engagement, you will be able to enter into a silent space inside yourself. This space is similar to what British psychoanalyst Donald W. Winnicott describes as "being alone in the presence of"[9] and is perhaps analogous to what is meant by the phrase commonly used by Christians to describe our relationship to the world, "being in the world but not of it" (see John 17:14-16).

This solitude of the heart can be experienced in the most unlikely places and circumstances. An article in a local paper profiles a sixty-nine-year-old nun of the Medical Mission Sisters who has found her "desert" in a group house of recovering alcoholics and drug addicts in the heart of the city.[10] Sister Margaret McKenna of Philadelphia had sought the desert while she was studying in Israel, spending a day a month in prayer in the desert between Jericho and Jerusalem. Now, however, her "desert" is a pair of row houses that serve as the residence of thirty recovering drug and alcoholic substance abusers in a section of the city where sixty percent of the houses are abandoned. Sister Margaret claims her own desert on a daily basis by meditating on the psalms and spending time in centering prayer. Her experience demonstrates that one's "desert," one's solitude of the heart, can be lived out in what would seem to be unfavorable circumstances. As Thomas Merton has written:

> To love solitude and to seek it does not mean constantly traveling from one geographical possibility to another. A man becomes a solitary at the moment when, no matter what may be his external surroundings, he is suddenly aware of his own inalienable solitude.... From that moment, solitude is not potential—it is actual.[11]

QUESTIONS FOR REFLECTION

1. The first step in claiming solitude is to give yourself permission. Would you say that you have given yourself permission? What factors—internal or external—do you see as affecting your ability to do so?

2. What practical arrangements do you need to make in order to prepare for a time of solitude? Which are the most difficult to resolve? What resources are available to help you?

3. Have you ever experienced "a solitude of the heart" while in the midst of other people? When and under what circumstances? Which ways of practicing

solitude have you found helpful in increasing your ability to experience a solitude of the heart?

4. Have you developed a rule of life that incorporates solitude? If so, what are the defining elements of your rule? If not, how could begin to form one now?

CHAPTER NINE

Sunfish Pond

E very two or three months I set aside a day to go to my special place, Sunfish Pond, four miles up the Appalachian Trail at the Delaware Water Gap on the Pennsylvania-New Jersey border. Throughout my life I have had a series of special places. When I was very young it was a fifty-foot-wide stretch of woods with a small stream next to the apartment house where we lived. A few years later, when I was old enough to get around town on my own, my special place was the Turtle Road woods, several hundred acres of forest with a field of goldenrod and a pond at its center. As a young adult living in Southern California, it was an undeveloped valley near our house, where the brown California hills rolled away toward the horizon. For the past several years and at this particular stage of my life, my special place is the Delaware Water Gap.

Special places where I can enter the silence and solitude and can touch the core of my being have always been important for me and for my spirituality. It is not always literally going *to* the special place that is important. It is simply knowing that it is there. Months may go by between visits. But simply knowing the special place is there nourishes my soul.

To get to the Delaware Water Gap from my house in the suburbs west of Philadelphia, I negotiate an hour and three-quarters of heavy traffic. Leaving early in the morning, I skirt the rush hour traffic into Philadelphia. An hour later I encounter heavy road construction outside Allentown before finally arriving at the Gap. I wonder if in some way the difficulties involved in getting to the Water Gap are actually an important part of the experience. The Hebrew people journeyed forty years through the wilderness. Elijah traveled through that same wilderness to Horeb, the mount of God. Paul journeyed to Arabia. Even people who live in highly desirable parts of the country tend to go elsewhere on vacation. Perhaps the journey *to* someplace is part of the spiritual journey. We each seem to sense that we have to put some space, some actual distance, between where we live our day-to-day lives and where we experience spiritual and emotional renewal.

Almost two hours after I leave I pull into the parking lot of the Water Gap Diner. I go inside and order breakfast: two scrambled eggs, home fries, sausage, and whole-wheat toast. This is part of the routine of the day. Later I will come back to this same restaurant and have a cup of coffee and a blueberry muffin. This too is part of the routine. What is it about routine that seems to be an important part of time alone and of renewal? Could it be that the very predictability of any ritual helps to "frame" the spiritual experience?

As I wait for my breakfast I look around the restaurant. A man in his twenties in jeans, work boots, and a baseball cap is talking to the waitress. A group of older men is sharing reminiscences in a booth. These are local people. Most of them, I suspect, have gone to school together, work together, and have married each other's sisters and daughters, brothers and sons. Their way of life has more in common with that of rural communities in western Pennsylvania and Ohio hundreds of miles to the west than it does with that of the New York suburbs only an hour east. As I look around I notice that I am only one of seven non-smokers. The smokers outnumber us at least three to one. This is exactly the reverse of what it would be among the health-conscious suburbanites with whom I live and minister. It reminds me that I am in another culture up here. In fact, entering this other culture and leaving my own behind for a day is part of the distancing—the "space"—that I seek when I come here.

My destination today is Sunfish Pond, a small, glaciated lake four miles up the Appalachian Trail. Having a destination is very important to me. Simply wandering around in the woods would not really satisfy what I am looking to experience. I like to know I am going *to* somewhere in my times alone. What is this importance of a destination when I seek silence and solitude? Is this part of my work ethic, I ask myself, that I have to have some "reason" for my excursion? Or is it something more? The Hebrew people wandered in the wilderness but they wandered for a reason: they were going to the Promised Land. Those undertaking a pilgrimage during the Middle Ages—or today—are going *to* a particular destination. I go to Sunfish Pond. There is something about a destination that tends to validate a spiritual journey.

I finish my breakfast, pay the bill, and drive the last couple of miles down the interstate to the parking lot at the entrance to the Appalachian Trail. My companion for the day is, as always, Molly, our irrepressible Labrador-Golden Retriever. Molly has proven herself on numerous occasions to be the ultimate trail dog, eagerly bounding up the path ahead of me or staying behind to investigate some fascinating natural phenomenon and then charging back up the trail. Besides enjoying Molly's companionship, I am privileged to see God's created order through Molly's eyes, expressing as she does that quality mentioned in the post-baptismal prayer of the Episcopal Church: "The gift of joy and wonder in all [God's] works" (BCP 308). I cannot imagine not having a dog along for a walk in the woods. During those rare periods in my life when I have been without a dog, I have always wished I could rent a dog for a half-day or a day for a walk in the woods.

This particular morning I decide to follow the Dunnfield Hollow Trail, which wanders through a shaded valley beside a mountain stream and then gradually climbs toward Sunfish Pond. I could also choose to follow the Appalachian Trail itself, which leads more directly toward the pond, or the Red Dot

Trail, which climbs to the top of Mt. Tammany, overlooking the Delaware River. The choice of trails on a
particular day is guided by the Holy Spirit and determined by some congruence between internal and
external reality. Author John Haines has written,
"The physical domain of the country had its coun-
terpart in me. The trails I made lead outward into the
hills and swamps, but they led inward also.... In
time the two become one in my mind."[1]

To approach Sunfish Pond by any one of these
trails I will climb approximately one thousand feet,
from the four-hundred-foot elevation of the
Delaware River to the almost fourteen-hundred-foot
elevation of Sunfish Pond. I have found that the act
of climbing *up* seems to be important. I discovered
this a few years ago when I explored another section
of the Appalachian Trail that involved hiking *down*
from the parking lot to my destination in the valley
and then back up to the car again. There was something strangely unsatisfying about this experience. I
have to hike up, I concluded. I think of those passages in scripture referring to high places, such as "I
will lift up my eyes to the hills" (Psalm 121:1), of
Mount Horeb or even of Jerusalem itself, which was
located on the spiny ridge of Palestine well over three
thousand feet above neighboring Jericho to the
north. The archetype of the mountain seems to speak
to all of us on our spiritual journeys.

Once Molly and I leave the immediate vicinity of
the parking lot, we do not encounter a single other
person on the trail for several miles. I realize that, if
I were to continue five miles directly north on the
Appalachian Trail toward High Point, or five miles

due west toward the Delaware River, or five miles east up and over the Kittatinny Ridge, I might not see a single other person. This means that, for some brief indeterminable period of time, I could conceivably be the only human being in a radius of a hundred square miles—in spite of being a two-hour drive away from thirty million people and only seventy miles from two major metropolitan areas. This idea fascinates me. Undoubtedly being the only human being in a hundred square miles would send a more gregarious soul screaming out of the woods. To me it is one of the attractions of this place.

Sunfish Pond was carved out by the great North American glacier twelve to eighteen thousand years ago. It is in fact the first glacial feature that a hiker coming north on the Appalachian Trail would encounter. If I had approached the Water Gap from the south several thousand years ago, I would have seen a great wall of ice two thousand feet thick stretching across the horizon as far as I could see and extending back into what is now Canada thousands of miles to the north. Something about the wild legacy of this place intrigues me. Even when I come up in summer, enveloped by the forest green and delighted by the sight of the wild flowers in bloom, the wild history of the Water Gap is never far from my mind and speaks to something deep inside me.

I move at a brisk pace up the trail. I think better and I even pray better when I am in motion. Many sermons have been composed on these trails, many parish programs planned. What is this link between physical motion and spiritual and intellectual awareness? Those who meditate speak of the "walking prayer" as a form of contemplation. This link between movement and spirituality is not something we tend to emphasize in the church, where we expect people to sit still and have a spiritual experience. Are we afraid that if we speak too much about the beauty of God's creation our members will be tempted to worship the god of the golf course or the state parks? Nevertheless, there is some profound and important link between physical movement and spirituality.

As I move on up the trail, I find I have the urge frequently to stop and listen. What am I listening *for* exactly? I am not sure I could say. In fact, I suspect that listening *for* something is what we need to leave behind when we enter our solitude. After some time I find myself experiencing that state described by nineteenth-century novelist and naturalist W. H. Hudson: "a state of intense alertness and preparedness, which compels [one] to watch and listen and go silently and stealthily... like that of the... animals."[2] For me a large part of prayer is alert watching and listening. Sometimes I find myself spontaneously lifting my arms and standing with my palms raised in the traditional *orans* prayer posture. What is fascinating to me is that I was assuming this posture in the woods long before I knew that it was a traditional prayer posture or even that it had a name in Christian tradition. I find that standing like this, if only for a moment, helps me to focus my attention outside of myself and, ultimately, on God.

About noon I reach the southern end of Sunfish Pond. I utter a silent greeting to the pond where the trail breaks through the trees and then proceed up the west side to one of my favorite spots, a rock outcropping overlooking the lake. I clamber up and position myself on a large flat rock overlooking the lake, watching the pattern of ripples on the surface of the water. There seems to be no discernable pattern to the ripples, or at least none that I can make out. They move in widening arcs from west to east and from north to south, stirred by the wind. The only man-made sound is the distant hum of a plane; other than that, I can hear simply the nearby rustling of leaves. This rock outcropping on the shore of the lake is a holy place. It is what the Celts called a "thin place." I think of those words of Jacob after he has fled into the desert, "Surely the LORD is in this place" (Genesis 28:16).

After several minutes of sitting quietly on the rock gazing out onto the lake, I stir myself and rejoin the trail at the water's edge. I follow it to another one of my favorite places, an area of stone monuments at the northern end of the lake. Over the years hikers have piled stones atop each other until today there are dozens of Stonehenge-like edifices. They stand silently facing the sun as it circles the lake. Some of these monuments are very simple: a few small stones piled together. Others are highly elaborate: two large columns of stones bridged by a flat, horizontal tablet, forming a dolmen, or stone table, one of humankind's earliest religious artifacts. Undoubtedly many of the anonymous hikers who constructed them would not consider themselves to be religious in any conventional sense at all. What, then, is this impulse to pile stone upon stone? What longing is being expressed? Furthermore, these stones all face the light of the sun. I discovered this one winter day as I watched a line of water melted by the warmth of the sun advancing in the direction of the stone monuments. The fact is, light appears to be significant in most religious traditions, including our own. How do these monument builders know to build them *here,* at this particular sun-washed end of the lake?

After a couple of hours at the pond, it is time for me to go. I hike the trail back the four miles to the parking lot. I make my usual stop at the diner for coffee and a blueberry muffin, and to reflect on the day's events. The traffic is heavy on the interstate as I cross into Pennsylvania, then on to Allentown, where once again I encounter the road construction. I realize that, at this time of day, I will probably hit the late afternoon rush hour traffic from Philadelphia. No matter. I have claimed my space. I have experienced my silence and solitude. I have been emotionally and spiritually renewed. I have once again met Christ in the silence and solitude of Sunfish Pond, and it is to this that I must return from time to time. I may not come back for many months, but I will revisit it often in my mind. The spirit of Sunfish Pond, the silence and solitude and the felt presence of God, will nourish my soul in the days and weeks ahead.

QUESTIONS FOR REFLECTION

1. Do you have a special place where you go periodically to renew yourself? Where is it? Are there common elements in the special places you have had throughout life?

2. Is physical distancing an important part of personal renewal for you? In what ways does the journey help prepare you for renewal? What other forms of distancing have you found helpful?

3. During periods of renewal in solitude, what routine do you follow? Does your routine tend to evolve and change as you enter more deeply into the solitude? How does your routine enable you to achieve a good solitude?

4. Have you experienced a link between physical activity and spiritual receptivity? When and under what circumstances? What physical activities bring you closer to a sense of God's presence?

Endnotes

CHAPTER 1
THE LOSS OF SOLITUDE

1. Jacob Needleman, *Time and the Soul* (New York: Doubleday, 1998), 60.
2. Anthony Storr, *Solitude: A Return to the Self* (New York: Ballantine Books, 1988), 5-6.
3. Doris Grumbach, *Fifty Days of Solitude* (Boston: Beacon Press, 1994), 22, 25-26.
4. *The Book of Common Prayer*, hereafter BCP, 268.
5. Anne Morrow Lindbergh, *Gift From the Sea* (New York: Vintage/Random House, 1965/1955), 30.
6. Ester Schaler Buchholz, *The Call of Solitude: Alonetime in a World of Attachment* (New York: Simon & Schuster, 1997), 20.

CHAPTER 2
THE DANGERS OF SOLITUDE

1. Buchholz, *Call of Solitude*, 29.
2. Storr, "Enforced Solitude," a chapter in *Solitude: A Return to the Self*, 42-61.

3. Robert D. Putnam, "Bowling Alone: America's Declining Social Capital," in *Journal of Democracy* 6, (January 1995): 65-78.

4. Grumbach, *Fifty Days of Solitude,* 22, 24.

5. Ibid., 35, 36.

6. Ibid., 105.

7. Doris Grumbach, *The Presence of Absence: On Prayers and an Epiphany* (Boston: Beacon Press, 1998), 119.

8. John A. Sanford and George Lough, *What Men Are Like* (New York: Paulist Press, 1988), 124.

9. C. G. Jung, *Memories, Dreams, Reflections* (London: Collins/Fontana, 1972), 214.

CHAPTER 3

THE HEALING POWER OF SOLITUDE

1. Susan Hertog, *Anne Morrow Lindbergh* (New York: Doubleday, 1999), 427.

2. Frederick Buechner. *The Longing for Home* (San Francisco: HarperCollins, 1996), 8.

3. Margaret Guenther, *Toward Holy Ground: Spiritual Directions for the Second Half of Life* (Cambridge, Mass.: Cowley Publications, 1995), 38.

4. James Gleick, *Faster: The Acceleration of Just About Everything* (New York: Pantheon, 1999), 277.

5. Theophan the Recluse, quoted by Timothy Ware, ed., in *The Art of Prayer: An Orthodox Anthology* (Boston: Faber & Faber, 1978), 234.

6. Henri J. M. Nouwen, *The Genesee Diary* (Garden City, N. Y.: Image/Doubleday, 1981), 81.

7. David S. Awbrey, *Finding Hope in the Age of Melancholy* (New York: Little, Brown, 1999), 28.

8. William Styron, *Darkness Visible: A Memoir of Madness* (New York: Random House, 1990), 69.

9. The forms of spirituality described in this section of the chapter are summarized by Alan H. Sager in *Gospel-*

Centered Spirituality: An Introduction to Our Spiritual Journey (Minneapolis: Augsburg Fortress, 1990), 30-56, based upon a phenomenology of spirituality articulated by Urban T. Holmes III (with John H. Westerhoff) in *A History of Christian Spirituality* (Philadelphia: Westminister, 1984).
10. Henri J. M. Nouwen, *The Way of the Heart: Desert Spirituality and Contemporary Ministry* (San Francisco: HarperCollins, 1981), 26-27.
11. Ibid., 44.

CHAPTER 4
SOLITUDE AND THE SELF
1. Mitch Albom, *Tuesdays with Morrie* (New York: Doubleday, 1997), 65-66.
2. Paul Hawker, *Soul Survivor: A Spiritual Quest Through 40 Days and 40 Nights of Mountain Solitude* (Kelowna, British Columbia: Northstone, 1998), 16-17.
3. Ibid, 128.
4. Joan Anderson, *A Year by the Sea: Thoughts of an Unfinished Woman* (New York: Doubleday/Random House, 1999), 38.
5. Kenneth Leech, *True Prayer: An Invitation to Christian Spirituality* (New York, Harper & Row, 1980), 176-177.
6. Richard Rohr, *Everything Belongs: The Gift of Contemplative Prayer* (New York: Crossroad Publishing, 1999), 44.
7. Lindbergh, *Gift from the Sea*, 23-24.
8. Gerald O'Collins, *The Second Journey: Spiritual Awareness and the Mid-Life Crisis* (New York: Paulist Press, 1978), 46.
9. Nouwen, *Genesee Diary*, 109.

CHAPTER 5

SOLITUDE AND TEMPERAMENT

1. See *Gifts Differing* by Isabel Briggs Myers, with Peter B. Myers (Palo Alto: Consulting Psychologists Press, 1980); and *Please Understand Me: An Essay on Temperament Styles* by David Keirsey and Marilyn Bates (Del Mar, Calif.: Prometheus Nemesis Books, 1978).

2. Theophan the Recluse, quoted in Ware, ed., *Art of Prayer,* 235.

3. Storr, *Solitude: A Return to the Self,* 143.

4. Buchholz, *Call of Solitude,* 46.

CHAPTER 6

SOLITUDE AND THE LIFE CYCLE

1. Nadya Labi, "Burning Out at Nine?", *Time* (November 23, 1998), 86. See also the reports of a study of time diaries of children age twelve and under from 1981 to 1997, conducted by the University of Michigan's Institute for Social Research and reported by Labi in "Burning Out at Nine?" and by Romesh Ratnesar in "The Homework Ate My Family: Kids are Dazed, Parents are Stressed," *Time* (January 25, 1999), 56.

2. Polly Berrien Berends, "Growing Together," *Spirituality and Health* (Fall, 1998), 32-33.

3. Gretchen A. Haertsch, in "No Time for Fun," *The Philadelphia Inquirer* (September 4, 1999).

4. John P. Robinson and Geoffrey Godbey, *Time for Life: The Surprising Ways Americans Use Their Time,* cited by Michael Sokolove in "Time Bandits," *Inquirer Magazine* of *The Philadelphia Inquirer* (September 20, 1998), 14.

5. Paul Tournier, *The Seasons of Life* (Atlanta: John Knox Press, 1963), 54.

6. Roger L. Gould, *Transformation: Growth and Change in Adult Life* (New York: Simon & Schuster, 1978), 310-311.

7. Robert Johnson, *He* (King of Prussia, Penn.: Religious Publishing Co., 1974), 80.

8. Lynne M. Baab, *Embracing Midlife: Congregations as Support Systems* (Bethesda, Md.: The Alban Institute, 1999), excerpted in *Congregations* (November/December 1999), 4.

9. Tim Stafford, *As Our Years Increase: Loving, Caring, Preparing for Life Past 65* (New York: HarperCollins, 1989), 79-102.

10. Mary C. Morrison, author of *Let Evening Come: Reflections on Aging,* quoted by Art Carey, columnist, in "At 88, She Celebrates the Gifts of Old Age," *The Philadelphia Inquirer* (March 3, 1999).

CHAPTER 7
SOLITUDE AND THE PRESENCE OF GOD
1. Grumbach, *Presence of Absence,* 3.
2. Buchholz, *Call of Solitude,* 65.

CHAPTER 8
RECLAIMING SOLITUDE
1. A. A. Milne, *The House at Pooh Corner* (New York: E. P. Dutton, 1928), 177.

2. Jessamyn West, *Hide and Seek,* quoted in Grumbach, *Fifty Days of Solitude,* 56-57.

3. Marsha Sinetar, *Ordinary People as Monks and Mystics: Lifestyles for Self-discovery* (New York: Paulist Press, 1984), 40-42.

4. Nouwen, *Genesee Diary,* 14.

5. Richard E. Byrd, *Alone* (New York: G. P. Putnam's Sons, 1938), 7, 160.

6. Jung, *Memories, Dreams, Reflections,* 199.

7. See Chester P. Michael and Marie C. Norrisey, *Prayer and Temperament: Different Prayer Forms for Different*

Personality Types (Charlottesville: The Open Door, Inc., 1984).
8. A. R. Weshart, *Monks and Monasteries* (Trenton: Albert Brandf, 1900), cited in Buchholz, *Call of Solitude*, 64.
9. Quoted by Anthony Storr in *Solitude: A Return to the Self,* 26.
10. Mary Beth McCauley, "In the Vineyards of Prayer: Nun Finds Her 'Desert' in N. Philadelphia," *The Philadelphia Inquirer* (November 7, 1999).
11. Thomas Merton, *Thoughts in Solitude* (New York: Farrar, Straus and Giroux, 1999), 77.

CHAPTER 9
SUNFISH POND
1. John Haines, *The Stars, the Snow, the Fire: Twenty-Five Years in the Northern Wilderness,* quoted by Jon Krakauer, *Into the Wild* (New York: Villard, 1996), 127.
2. W. H. Hudson, *Idle Days in Patagonia* (London: Chapman and Hall, 1893), 230.

Resources

Anderson, Joan. *A Year by the Sea: Thoughts of an Unfinished Woman*. New York: Doubleday/ Random House, 1999.

Buchholz, Ester Schaler. *The Call of Solitude: Alonetime in a World of Attatchment*. New York: Simon & Schuster, 1997.

Byrd, Richard E. *Alone*. New York: G. P. Putnam's Sons, 1938.

France, Peter. *Hermits: The Insights of Solitude*. New York: St. Martin's Griffin, 1996.

Graham, Aelred. *Contemplative Christianity*. New York: The Seabury Press, 1974.

Grumbach, Doris. *Fifty Days of Solitude*. Boston: Beacon Press, 1994.

_____, *The Presence of Absence: On Prayers and an Epiphany*. Boston: Beacon Press, 1998.

Hawker, Paul. *Soul Survivor: A Spiritual Quest Through 40 Days and 40 Nights of Mountain*

Solitude. Kelowna, British Columbia, Canada: Northstone, 1998.

Henderson, Bill. *Tower: Faith, Vertigo, and Amateur Construction.* New York: Farrar, Straus and Giroux, 2000.

Hudson, W. H. *Idle Days in Patagonia.* London: Chapman & Hall, 1893.

Jung, C. G. *Memories, Dreams, Reflections.* London: Collins/Fontana, 1972.

Leech, Kenneth. *True Prayer: An Invitation to Christian Spirituality.* New York: Harper & Row, 1980.

Lindbergh, Anne Morrow. *Gift from the Sea.* New York: Vintage/Random House, 1965.

Merton, Thomas. *A Search for Solitude: Pursuing the Monk's True Life,* Lawrence S. Cunningham, ed. San Francisco: HarperSanFrancisco, 1996.

_____, *Thoughts in Solitude.* New York: Farrar, Straus and Giroux, 1999.

Michael, Chester P. and Marie C. Norrisey. *Prayer and Temperament: Different Prayer Forms for Different Personality Types.* Charlottesville: The Open Door, Inc., 1984.

Norris, Kathleen. *The Cloister Walk.* New York: Riverhead/Berkley, 1996.

Nouwen, Henri J. M. *Out of Solitude: Three Meditations on the Christian Life.* Notre Dame: Ave Maria Press, 1974.

_____, *The Genesee Diary.* Garden City, N.Y.: Image/Doubleday, 1981.

_____, *The Way of the Heart: Desert Spirituality and Contemporary Ministry.* New York: HarperCollins, 1981.

Sarton, May. *Journal of a Solitude.* New York: Norton, 1973.

Sinetar, Marsha. *Ordinary People as Monks and Mystics: Lifestyles for Self-discovery.* New York/ Mahwah: Paulist Press, 1986.

Storr, Anthony. *Solitude: A Return to the Self.* New York: Ballantine Books, 1988.

Ware, Timothy, ed. *The Art of Prayer: An Orthodox Anthology.* Boston: Faber & Faber, 1978.